GOLD DIGGERS, BEAN COUNTERS & "MISS MANAGEMENT"

TOO YOUNG TO RETIRE, TOO OLD TO CHANGE JOBS IN A HOSTILE WORK ENVIRONMENT

MACK STOUT

ISBN: 9781073029334

Cover Design by www.100covers.com
Interior Design by www.formattedbooks.com

DEDICATION

To K. N., who is quite honestly the best manager I have ever worked for, and to L. B., who, of all the managers I have worked for, is one of them. To the former, for making this book possible, to the latter, for making it necessary.

CONTENTS

FOREWORD   I

INTRODUCTION   V

1. OLD SCHOOL   1
2. ELIGIBLE TO HAVE A LIFE   17
3. SECOND-HAND SMOKE   35
4. RECOVERY   50
5. FINDING A HOME   63
6. THE NEW NORMAL   77
7. RED SKY AT MORNING   93
8. ENTER MISS MANAGEMENT   107
9. FIGHT OR FLIGHT   123
10. RED SKY AT NIGHT   138
11. RHYMES WITH DUCK FAT   157

CONCLUSION   172

ACKNOWLEDGMENTS   183

ABOUT THE AUTHOR   185

FOREWORD

By Heywood Jablomie

Mack Stout was born to tell this story.

I have known Mack for many years, and if there is one characteristic about him that stands out, it is the fact that he is a man of few words. I can tell when something is eating at him, and I do my best to draw him out at those times to see what is really going on. It usually comes down to his frustrations with the people with whom he lives and works, and how they act in ways that make a sane person wonder why they subject themselves to this kind of behavior. I have often lent a sympathetic ear when he just needs to vent.

I mentioned to him once that he should write a book about his struggles with co-workers, and he said that he had thought about it, but he was afraid that stories like "Game of Thrones" or "Zombie Apocalypse" would be warmer, fuzzier, and more believable, and anyway, who would ever want to read a book like that? I told him to think about the times when he struggled to make it through another day in the situations he had experienced, and I asked him whether it would have helped if he could have learned from the experiences of someone who had gone through something similar? He started to see that there could be value in talking about some of these experiences.

While I was helping him edit this book, he expressed concern that maybe he should tone down the language a bit. I told him he should read the memoir by the late, great Carrie Fisher, "The Princess Diarist." I had no idea Princess Leia could be such a potty-mouth. He said "that may be, but Carrie Fisher is famous, and I am not." I told him. "that is all the more reason for people to be interested. In an era when people can become famous for being famous, you can be notable for being ordinary. One thing you definitely are is relatable." There are a lot of people out there who work for horrible bosses who could gain some useful perspective on how to deal with it.

The other thing about Mack that is amazing is his ability to re-call details of occurrences after many years have passed. I men-tioned after reading some of his anecdotes that I would love to sift through his journals and diaries, and he said he never keeps any. In his mind, the only people who benefit from diaries are blackmailers, so he prefers to commit it all to memory. In fact, he said that if your journals aren't of interest to blackmailers and extortionists, then you probably don't have anything worth journaling about. I asked his friends and relatives about the ac-curacy of some of these stories, and without exception, they report that it is all accurate. So, while I know Mack can forgive, I now know that he also rarely forgets[1].

1   So don't fuck with him.

Mack's sense of humor may well be an acquired taste for many, but for someone who describes his life as either a light tragedy or a dark comedy depending on how you look at it, he has found a way to accentuate the humor. Always one to see the silver lining in any cloud or the light at the end of every tunnel, he is a great example of making lemonade out of life's lemons. He can even see the humor in an emergency appendectomy (and yes, it was his own), so I would say he can lighten up with the best of them. One thing I constantly bring him up short on is his tendency to go off on rants. Mack has some axes to grind, and the most common target of his rants tend to be pretentious people, people who are preachy, and millennials. If you happen to be a pretentious, preachy millennial, consider yourself warned.

I often feel like my role in Mack's inner circle of acquaintances is to serve as Devil's Advocate, that is, to challenge his opinions and beliefs to make sure he really has the courage of his convictions. He usually stands his ground admirably, and I would trust his judgments without reservation. Mack has told me that he considers himself to be a no-nonsense type of person, but sometimes, nonsense is the only way to make sense of this nonsense. So, sit back, relax, and enjoy the ride through this theater of the absurd, and realize that it could happen to you too.

Note: Heywood Jablomie is a close friend of Mack's and a trusted confidant. This is not his real name, although the letters in his real name could be rearranged to spell "Photon Bombs."

INTRODUCTION

As people go through their careers, they will be subjected to behaviors from co-workers and superiors that run counter to their own values and beliefs. The choice is whether to tolerate these behaviors, seek to correct them, or to move on to a different situation. I have always been one of those people who never rock the boat, and I keep my opinions to myself for the sake of keeping the peace and staying employed. I have never been fired from a job, and, in fact, I usually stay with a job way longer than any self-respecting person would, mainly because I despise the process of looking for work. In retrospect, I have to ask myself just how much is too much, and why did I subject myself to these behaviors for the sake of continuing to have a job.

If you find yourself in a situation where you are surrounded by people who have gamed the system to their advantage, or who justify their existence by questioning the value of yours, or just generally dread the thought of going in to work to face an abusive boss for one more day, then you need to figure out a way to change your life. Please note that I have just listed the types of people for whom this book is named, and I have encountered them all. From the little honey who dreams of being able to say

"I married the boss, now I can get fat," the opportunist who sees your position as a threat and looks to convince the powers that be that your work could be farmed out overseas at a fraction of the cost, thereby, freeing up resources that could be headed his way, to the power player who wants to eliminate the deadwood and get rid of undesirables. Hopefully, by learning from my experiences, you will get the motivation and belief that you can make this change.

This is the story of how I came to understand that too many people trade their passion for an existence out of a sense of duty or obligation to family and friends and end up unfulfilled and riddled with regrets later in life, never realizing that they are not being fair to one key individual in their lives, namely, themselves. So, I embarked on a journey to find opportunity, fulfillment, and validation, and what I got was a life dominated by gold diggers, bean counters, and Miss Management.

Every now and then, the thought occurs to me that the more time that passes since I have removed myself from a bad situation, the better it feels. In my case, many of these situations involve jobs I have had, mostly from my days in the software industry. From time to time, I have awakened from a dream where I was back working for any number of my former bosses and have had the feeling of overwhelming relief that it was only a dream. If you have ever faced the prospect of reliving days spent working for a horrible boss, or just a work situation where you were not a good fit, then you know what I am talking about.

For many years, the model of the American Dream has been

to get a good education and find a job that has the potential to pay a high salary. Then buy the biggest house on which you can keep the payments current and a new car every few years so that you have something to show for all your hard work. The conventional wisdom was that by doing this, you would somehow be better off than your parents. People have been buying into this argument of conforming to society's expectations for decades. The reality is that for many of us, a job is just that. A place to while away 40 hours a week at varying degrees of productivity followed by a period of time known as the weekend. This is characterized by spending Friday evening recovering from the rigors of the workweek, Saturday catching up on tasks needing to be performed and possibly doing something for yourself and/or your family, and Sunday dreading the arrival of Monday morning and starting the whole cycle over again. If this sounds depressing, welcome to my world.

According to data from the U.S. Census Bureau, in 1950, the share of the population over age 25 who had completed college was just above 5%. By 2015, that share had risen to over 25%.[2] Clearly, the message was getting through that college was the way to achieve success, although there are alternatives, such as learning a trade and entrepreneurship. I recall reading a statement that said the best way to achieve success is to provide a useful product or service for which people are willing and able to pay. If you can accomplish this feat by doing something that you enjoy and are passionate about, it is a major victory. Too many of us spend our lives selling our productive time to a business that doesn't appreciate us for what we can do, only for what

2   U.S Census Bureau 1947 – 2015 Current Population Survey and 1940 Decennial Census.

we will do for them. We end up like the Jack Nicholson character in the movie "About Schmidt," who worked for a big insurance company his whole life, and on his last afternoon before he retires, spends the time in his empty office staring at the clock on the wall waiting for the afternoon to end. Presumably, he had many such similar afternoons, but at least with the appearance of a purpose to his being there.

Other than to provide background information, I am only relating here experiences I have had in the workplace since graduating from college. Everything I tell about in these pages actually happened during my time with various employers and my own entrepreneurial endeavors. In most cases, the names have been changed to provide plausible deniability, and to allow time for some royalties to pile up in case I need to move to South America. The who and where and when are not that important. This could happen to anyone, anywhere, at any time. If it is happening to you, you need to establish your threshold of abuse and set your boundaries. If you are one of these horrible bosses, and you see yourself in the accounts that follow, simply understand that the descriptions that I relate here serve to explain how your actions impacted my life, and my reactions to them. If you feel some guilt or remorse at causing these reactions, well, all I can say is that it is a wise person who can see himself or herself and admit it.

What is the value of a college degree? To many employers, it shows that you are teachable and will put up with tremendous amounts of bullshit to accomplish a desired goal, which it could be argued, is all that attaining a bachelor's degree demonstrates. Then, too, that is all that some employers are interested in. They may not want too many employees who are astute enough to challenge the status quo. There are, of course, those students who work diligently and apply themselves to a specific purpose, but there are also those who goof off and party their way through school and are nowhere near ready to face the challenges of a career when they are handed their diploma.

The trajectory of your life is often a product of where you started. For me, I came from a small rural community and wasn't shown much to which to aspire to in life. Since I was the youngest of four boys in my family, I ended up thinking that I had to settle for other people's leavings. My youngest older brother, who is 13 years older than I am, sought to better his situation by getting away from that environment as soon as he possibly could. He went to college and moved to an area where jobs in his chosen field were plentiful and paid well. Since my parents were children of the Great Depression, they preached that just having a job was the most important thing, and that following passions and dreams were luxuries that were not necessarily available to everyone.

While much of this book concerns my struggles at work over the years, I have also included many of the stories of the things that make it all worthwhile, like adventures experienced in my travels on vacation trips and time spent enjoying peace and quiet at home with my family and my cats. There is a lot to be said for a work-life balance.

If I had to come up with a one-word description for myself, it would have to be pragmatic. It is, without a doubt, my super-power. While those around me can indulge in thoughts of thrift, spirituality, and high-minded philosophical interests, it has always been my lot to figure out how to put my feet on the floor and get the damn thing done. While I would love to be able to stand my ground on principles of traditional down-home values, I know that I need to operate within the constraints of my surroundings. To do so without abandoning my core beliefs is a never-ending challenge.

A word of warning. While I have attempted to keep the language and descriptions of this account as family-friendly as possible, the fact is that it is easy to become maxed out living and working around those who exhibit a never-ending parade of character flaws and those whose lives resemble a toxic trash dumpster fire, and I want to present it as accurately as I can recall. Therefore, in the recent words of one such individual in an infamous social media post, if I can't un-see this, neither can you.

Another thing I should say at the outset is, if you are put off by a perceived lack of political correctness in the title of this work, then I would like to say I'm sorry. That is, I would like to, but I can't. Don't get me wrong, I am as sensitive and socially aware as anyone, and I have seen the effects of blindly following social conventions because that is the way things have always been done. I understand how people can get a stick up their butt about it, but in my mind, the pendulum has swung a bit too far the other way. There is a comedian I have heard named Brad

Stine who said that he wants to see political correctness die in his lifetime, but first, he wants to see it suffer. Well, this might be a good start.

OLD SCHOOL

1

IT HAS BEEN A LONG ROAD, AND MOST OF IT WAS SURFACED WITH
gravel. Those are words that I have heard my oldest brother use
to describe life for those of us who do not come from a background of wealth and status. I heard him say a lot of things that
may or may not be true, but for some reason, this one has stood
out in my mind. One of the disadvantages of being the youngest sibling is that everyone else in the family has witnessed most
of my moments of which I would rather not be reminded, but I
haven't really seen that many of theirs. And I'm told there were
some whoppers.

The road was not only long and rough but winding. After a
few years of relative calm, I suddenly came to a disturbing realization: I was in a situation where I had begun aging out of a
career path I chose many years ago. On top of that, since the

company where I had been working more or less contentedly for several years had been acquired by its biggest competitor, I was now working for a manager who could best be described as a millennial with an agenda. Part of that agenda was to see if she could teach new tricks to old dogs, and, it appeared, had decided going in that the answer was no. So, I felt like I was being targeted by my manager for treatment that was 'encouraging' me to move on.

The truth is, I have never really been in a job situation where I felt comfortable or secure. I had jobs where I worked for people who lacked emotional stability, tact, and good character in general. I know that a lot of people never would have tolerated the situations I was in for any length of time. But it never occurred to me that I could do anything about it, either because of my work ethic or just the thought that this was the best thing I could find. A lot of that thinking had to do with my background and upbringing.

I grew up on a cattle ranch in an area that probably belongs in the National Register of Unfortunate Place Names, an expanse of prairie and farmland called Squaw Gap, North Dakota. If they made a movie that was set in this place, it might be called "A State Line Runs Through It." Coming from an area like this was like something out of the Andy Griffith Show, and I am about Ron Howard's age. The closest town of any size was 25 miles away on the other side of the state line, a state containing mountains and significant amounts of sky. It was an area of about 500 square miles with about 100 families. After years of battling what Ma Bell called too much red tape, it was the early 1970s before we even got phone service. The roads in our locale were not actually surfaced with gravel, but a form of reddish clay that is dug from deposits in hillsides around the nearby area. It is very soft and breaks up and pulverizes easily with the traffic on the roads over time. Once it does, any car or truck coming down the road kicks up a trail of dust that resembles the rocket cars that you may see running along the Bonneville Salt Flats in Utah, only at about $1/20^{th}$ the speed.

I went to a one-room country school through the eighth grade. Mrs. Rachel Schleur (not this person's real name, but the letters in her real name could be rearranged to spell "no non-simians") was the one and only teacher I had for my eight years of elementary school. She was a typical schoolmarm if that means anything to someone under the age of 30 or so, and what she lacked in intellect, she made up for with orneriness. As for my schoolmates, during those eight years, the student population topped out at 14 when I was in fourth grade. Along the way, for most of those years, my nemesis was a demented hillbilly clan with three boys and a girl who more or less made my life a living hell. They finally moved away before my last year there, and it was only myself and my three nephews in the school. Finally, I reached the top of the pecking order, but I think I had the grace to not press my advantage.

During my time in grade school, one of the big things that interested me was the space program. I was too young to have really been aware of much during the Mercury days, except that

I knew mom had a great deal of admiration for John Glenn. By the time the space race got into full swing with the Gemini program, I was hooked on watching as much coverage on television as I could. I don't think I ever actually thought that I could become an astronaut, either because I was somehow aware that only a select few could hope to be chosen for such an exclusive calling or, most likely, because I knew that mom would never let me get near an actual rocket. She was the biggest worry-wart that ever lived, and I spent much of my childhood being stifled by her over-protective nature. I know she meant well, but I think it is fair to say that a sheltered existence can stunt your growth.

One of my favorite escapes or distractions in those days was watching cartoons on TV, and my favorite was Popeye the Sailor. In Popeye's world, there was no challenge that couldn't be overcome by spinach-fueled fists of fury. Unfortunately, I never did learn to develop a taste for canned spinach, so I'm afraid that I probably wouldn't have gone far on Popeye's crew, since in his words, "anybody what don't like spinach is my em-in-ee." Nowadays, his bravado would probably be seen as promoting 'toxic masculinity,' and I admit, I probably wouldn't want my kids to watch him, but I turned out alright.

Life in a rural farming community had its benefits in that it was a fairly close-knit group of people, and we all looked after each other. The lack of phone service was a challenge at times, but we worked around it. Like that Friday in late November of 1963, when I was out on the schoolyard during lunch hour and saw a cloud of dust coming down the road from about a mile away. The car stopped at the schoolhouse, and a lady went in to talk to Mrs. Schleur; we were called in and given the news of the events unfolding in Dallas that day. I was in first grade, and even then, I was well aware of the significance of this event, mainly because mom thought that JFK was the reincarnation of Saint FDR. Apparently, she didn't like Ike or people of Ike's ilk. We went home early and were glued to the TV for the rest of the weekend.

It is fair to say that the best thing I had going for me in those days was that I was surrounded by good examples of bad examples. Case in point, my oldest brother could, more or less, be described as the town drunk and the next youngest worked in law enforcement for a time, eventually rising to the position of undersheriff. It all made for some interesting dinner conversations, but that is a story for another day. I certainly never had anyone to guide me in the ways of successful people. But from the first time I saw my dad trudge out on a cold winter day and reach his arm up into the hindquarters of a heifer to hook a chain around her calf's leg to pull it out, I was pretty sure there must be a better way to make a living. I just never got a clear indication of what the economics of farming and ranching were, in the sense that I had no idea what the annual income was that we generated. We didn't have it that rough, considering that we had decent vehicles, appliances, and even indoor plumbing (which is something that the school house lacked), but as far as having an indication of what provided that, I was totally clueless. After my brother went off to college and a successful career, the remaining relatives I had in the area probably felt that, in my case, it would be good to keep expectations low, since if I ever amounted to anything, it might make them look bad. Some years later, I saw a movie where a mid-level executive was asked by a manager how much he made. The guy said something like $42,000, at which the manager gasped in horror and said, "but you're 47 years old. We have a rule here that anyone who isn't earning their age is a loser. That means you have been a loser for five years!" That was the first indication I had of society's expectations of what constitutes a respectable showing in the game of life. I heard later that the figure had moved to one and a half times a person's age, and I think it became double at some point. I shudder to think what it is now. I just tell people that I'm making close to six figures, five to be exact. That is my way of saying if I couldn't laugh, I would cry.

Moving on to high school in town was even worse than grade school as I didn't really fit into any of the cliques that were established there. They had jocks, hippies, and cowboys. That is a tough environment for a geeky kid from the wrong side of the tracks who lacked anything even remotely resembling self-confidence. Looking back on it, I really wish that some of the self-appointed advocates in the fight against bullying could have been there to see what I dealt with. I got through it somehow, but after four years of misery, I had my fill of school for a while. So, I took a job with the state department of revenue transferring data from property record cards to a format that could be entered on punch cards for computerized record keeping. After that was done, I took any job I could find because I remembered what my mom said, you have to take any job you can find.

Everyone said I should go to college, but they didn't say what I should study or what I could expect to accomplish by getting a degree. If I ever expressed an ambition, it was usually shot down by those who wanted to promote the belief that I couldn't pour water out of a boot if the instructions were printed on the heel.

Not long after I graduated high school, my mom discovered she had cancer and had to have major surgery. Dad wasn't really up to the task of taking care of her by himself, so I had to stay around and help out. (I'm being generous here, as the reality is that many of us thought he couldn't be trusted. He complained a bit that I was 'living at home' because he didn't want me around, but that had been the case for 20 years or more. When I found that out, it solidified my stand on certain social issues.) My parents finally got divorced about a year later within just a few days of my 21st birthday. I used to say the only reason they waited that long was that neither one of them wanted to risk getting custody of me.

I took a job at the sugar refinery in town, where I received a thorough indoctrination in the ways of labor unions. The factory was a strict union shop, and everything revolved around seniority, so if you didn't have that seniority, you didn't have… much. One interesting dynamic of this time was that during the late '70s and early '80s, there was a boom of oil well drilling activity in our area, and many of the people who had good jobs at the time eagerly left them to seek their fortune in the oil patch. It was a cycle that would be repeated over the decades, each time giving rise to the quip, "Lord, let the boom come back, I promise not to piss it away this time." Well, the one peculiar thing that happened during this early boom time was that even though the sugar factory had long been considered the best job opportunity in the local area, nevertheless, people gave no thought to leaving it behind to rake in the big bucks that awaited them on the rigs. Those who for whatever reason chose not to follow were rewarded with rapid advancement up the pay scale, and as a result, the average age of a foreman or shift superintendent when I came on was late 20s to early 30s. By the time it became apparent that the oil field jobs were not going to go on forever, all the folks who left found themselves having to start over at the bottom. Needless to say, very few of them opted for that choice, and instead, left the area or became bartenders.

A couple of years later, I moved to a nearby bigger city where I felt comfortable, mainly because no one there knew me. I started, once more, to search for a way to make my fortune (I still didn't have a clear idea of what exactly constituted a fortune) and once again started the cycle of job to job living. One thing this town had that had been unavailable where I lived before was a college. So, I thought, hey, I can live here and go to college, thereby, getting my friends and family off my back. I decided to study Accounting since that was the first thing listed in the school catalog.

Early on, I found college life not that difficult. There were adjustments to be made, but I was hopeful that I could handle the social aspect of it better than I had in high school. I checked out some of the organizations but still found it difficult to really embrace socializing. I got to know some of the business majors and started to feel I was moving in the right direction. By the end of the first year, I had dropped a class or two that I figured I could pick up later. About that time, my mom was having complications from her cancer surgery, and I felt the need to go home and help her out again. As they say, one thing leads to another, and I ended up getting my sugar factory job back while I was taking care of mom. School got pushed to the side, where it remained for a number of years.

After a couple of years of working seasonally, I was hired year-round. During this year, the factory was undergoing a major equipment upgrade, and they needed extra workers for the construction. So I began to experience life on a secure payroll, which through most of the '80s, was not such a bad place to be. I settled into a routine of working 8-5 Monday through Friday and having the weekend to relax. So, life was good, and I felt like I was on my way. By the end of the summer, the factory upgrade was complete, and we were off and running making sugar again. The steady routine of Monday through Friday gave way to 24/7 rotating shifts, which, in its own way, was a welcome change of pace; one I would, for the most part, come to enjoy over the next few years.

With opportunity limited at the top tier of the organization, it became a struggle to get a position among the intermediate level technicians. Some of us were able to advance, and I finally got a post to one of the key areas, even though my position was considered a secondary tech job. This was significant because one year during the collective bargaining negotiations, management decided that they were going to arbitrarily reassign workers from the factory floor to the warehouse at their sole discretion, for a comparatively lower wage. As you might imagine, that did not sit well with the union, and it very nearly resulted in a strike being called. As negotiations dragged on, a compromise was reached in which the foremen and primary technicians would be exempt from this structure. I bet you can't guess which group of employees made up the bulk of the negotiating committee. Did you guess the foremen and primary techs? Brilliant!

Once again, I decided to make the break from home and move back to the big city. By now, almost 10 years had passed since I was in college, but it was still there. That spring, I decided that it would be a good idea to go back and pick up the couple of classes that I needed to finish my freshman year and go at it full-bore in the fall. As luck would have it, I got a job at the end of that summer that was going to require me to drive all over the region for weeks at a time, so once again, school was going to have to wait. I ended up doing this job, which involved photographing students at elementary and high schools and being unemployed during the summer. In my free time, I started to pick up some photography assignments doing weddings and family pictures, and I entertained the idea of starting my own studio. My whole reason for taking the school picture job was because I had an interest in photography and thought it would be a good way to learn the craft. I was able to cobble together some equipment from the boss's junk bins and from a used camera store that was run by a pair of retired guys who liked to tinker with old equipment and had nothing better to do with their time. I was probably their favorite customer.

In my early days of learning the school picture business, I met a great lady named Maxine Mumm.[3] If my life were a dark comedy, hers would be a soap opera. When we met, she was a widow with two teenage boys and had been through the typical single mom trials and tribulations. Like me, she had been instilled early on with a life ethic that said you take responsibility for your situation and work hard to make a go of it. So, long story short, we got married the following summer, and I had a wife and two teenage sons to integrate into my life.

When the school picture season started that fall, it was business as usual until the end of the week before Thanksgiving. I returned from a typical week-long road trip and was not feeling very well. The next morning, I woke up covered with spots, and Maxine told me it appeared that I had a case of chicken pox. I guess that is an occupational hazard of someone who works around large numbers of young children and, who as a child, was not exposed to many children and their communicable diseases. That ended my season of work, and I got an extended Christmas vacation that year.

For the first four years of our marriage, I continued to do the school photography seasonal job and filled in with whatever side gigs I could manage to find along the way. At one point in the second half of my second year on the job, I had an epic

3　Just go with it.

meltdown that could very easily have ended my employment with that company. It seems as if each school has its own unique personality as far as the student's behavior and attitudes go, and there were some schools I loved going to. There were others I absolutely dreaded going to, because it seemed that the students, and in some cases, the teachers and administrators, were actively trying to be difficult. So, on one day at a school, I was working with another photographer at the beginning of a week-long road trip, a class of seventh graders was being excessively boisterous, and a piece of equipment got knocked over. Not a high-priced computerized camera, or a bank of strobe lights and reflectors. No, as I recall, it was a sign board that held press-on letters that we used to identify the group in the class pictures (about the most low-tech object in the room), but it was enough to put my stress level over the top, and I told them just exactly what I thought of them. The issue stemmed from the fact that I thought they were a bunch of f___ing little a__holes, and I wasn't shooting blanks if you know what I mean. Things got real quiet after that, and looking back on it, I really feel sorry for the photographer I was working with as it was his first year of being in the business[4]. We got back to the motel room that afternoon, and there was a message for me that I might want to contact my office. We had a discussion about what happened, and I was told that it might be a good idea if that didn't happen again. I have always believed that the boss realized what a difficult environment it was, and the fact was that the reason he hires photographers to go to these places is so that he doesn't have to do it himself. But he had a long-standing relationship

4   No, I didn't feel sorry for the seventh graders, because they were a bunch of f___ing little a__holes.

12

with the principal at the school, who I should point out was a very nice and easy-going person who just happened to be out-matched by the mob rule tendency there. Anyway, the only real consequence of this was that I had to write a letter of apology to the class and staff at the school. The other, and much worse, consequence was that he sent me back to that school the fol-lowing year, as he explained to me that whenever things at a picture day don't go as well as they could, he always sends that photographer back to show that he or she is truly great at what they do. I'm sure that they were as unconvinced of that as I was convinced that my only reason for being there was so that the boss didn't have to be.

After about seven years of trying to get a foothold in the local photography market, I realized that I was really only making enough money from the photography business to cover the bills that without it, I wouldn't have to worry about, I decided to take a job with the local newspaper running their vending machine routes. I began this job running the routes during the day to simply restock machines that were running out of papers and replace defective coin mechanisms. It was not unusual to find a hand-written 'out of order' sign taped to a machine, and of-ten, the only thing out of order was the operator. My favorite example of this was that on more than one occasion, I would find one of these signs on a rack on Sunday when the price of the paper went from 75 cents to $1.75. Keep in mind that this was a simple coin slot mechanism that was clearly designed to accept only quarters. But every now and then, I would find that someone had taken a dollar bill and folded it twice and pushed it through the slot, then jammed three quarters in after it. It helps you understand that the difference between genius and stupidity is that genius has its limits.

While I was working at the newspaper[5], one of my frequent stops was the college I had attended many years earlier, and it was starting to dawn on me that being a college drop-out wasn't working out quite as well for me as it did for Bill Gates. One thing I did get established that was making me some reliable cash was an annual gig running photo-finish cameras during the horse racing meets that ran several weekends each summer and fall. For some reason, the thought occurred to me that I could take that money and invest it in going back to school. It was enough to get me started that fall, and by jumping through all the necessary hoops, I was able to secure a stream of financial aid that would allow me to finally complete my degree program, which by this time, I had decided would be in computer information systems. It seemed like the sensible thing to pursue because I figured that the future was about computers, and with my social anxiety, I felt I would rather spend my time crunching numbers and lines of code than partying. While in my earlier days in school, I was fairly good at science, math was a different story. I don't think I ever worked as hard as I had the first couple of months that fall to be able to work algebra concepts, but it finally clicked, and soon, I was able to solve complex problems involving compound interest and statistical analysis. Maybe it finally got through to me that several people had mentioned to me that I seem to have a talent for being analytical. Maybe they meant anal-retentive and were just trying to be nice, but at any

5   The letters in the name of this newspaper could be rearranged to spell "Belittling Gazes"

rate, I started to apply myself to school like never before.

The head of the Information Technology Department, Dr. Anita Schauer (not this person's real name, but the letters in her real name could be rearranged to spell "yes, loiterer"), was a professor who had a bit of a rough exterior, but once you got to know her, you realized she was tough as nails. By my senior year, she had decided to retire at the end of the year, and people felt that she was losing her edge, in the sense that some people quit their jobs and left; it seems she quit and stayed.

Years earlier, when I had attended this school, I heard it said that you couldn't go anywhere out of state and get a job with a degree from this school. That was when the school was a small state college and mainly served the local market, which was fairly large. When I came back, the school had been assimilated into the state university system, and now I was hearing that there weren't really a lot of jobs available locally for people with their information systems degree, meaning that you would likely have to go out of state. The other discouraging words I heard were that employers really don't like to hire anyone over 40. I thought this odd, considering that this school seemed to cater to 'non-traditional' students, meaning those in the over 40 crowd, so it seemed that someone must think it is a worthwhile endeavor. After three very intense years of being maxed out on course loads each semester and taking summer classes and CLEP tests to fill in gaps in my transcript, I finally achieved my goal of attaining a bachelor's degree. At the age of 43. Little did I realize that while I thought I had just given myself an edge in my career prospects, I was embarking on a path that would make the Dilbert Zone look like a shining example of well-run efficiency. Or, in another of my brother's keen analyses, I would be going through deep shit on a short horse.

ELIGIBLE TO HAVE A LIFE

2

I LEFT MY JOB AT THE NEWSPAPER DURING MY LAST SEMESTER AT college to concentrate on finals and to take a bit of a breather. After a few weeks of looking for meaningful work, I landed a job unloading trucks before dawn for a local big box type store. This went on for a few weeks, and eventually, I was called by a temp agency to interview for a job with what was purported to be a local tech company. With credentials at the ready, I confidently walked into the offices of AFAHM Services Inc. (not this company's actual name, but for reasons that will be made clear later, that is how I will refer to it). I sat at a conference table with the owner, Chris Chan (not this person's real name but you could rearrange the letters in his real name to spell "nearsighted lice")[6], the office manager Marion DeBos (who would turn out to be the owner's wife), and the bookkeeper. Mr. Chan said that he chose the name of the company from a list of possibilities

6   Although I can't begin to imagine why anyone would want to.

that a college friend who was in marketing had put together for him, and he chose the first name on the list. I understood. The job was explained as being about maintaining a help desk system built on an Access database program. I was intrigued. It was just a couple of years earlier that I had taken Dr. Shauer's Microcomputer Database class. This was during the summer session, so it was a condensed version of the class, but I really applied myself and spent a lot of time outside of school working on it, at one point, practically rebuilding it from the ground up to get it right. So, it sounded like the ideal situation for me.

The owner of the business was a commanding presence. He seemed secure in the knowledge that his business was successful and growing. It was essentially a company that handled third-party repair and maintenance for computers, printers, and other specialized technology, such as the modems that powered ATMs for banks. They had clients nationwide and contracted with local tech businesses to provide a technician to go to the customer's site and perform the repairs. This obviously required negotiating a discounted rate with the provider so that the difference would be the fee collected by the third-party broker. It turned out that some techs were more willing than others to work for these terms. More on that later.

During my first week in the company, I suddenly realized that I had gone to college with Chris years ago when I made my first run at higher education. I was not well acquainted with him, but we did have some mutual friends, among them was the marketing guy who came up with the list of potential names for his company. I also found out that he and Marion, who had been working for the company for a while, had married recently. Thus, I became familiar with what can best be described as the phenomenon of the gold digger. I'm not so hopelessly old fashioned and naïve that I frown on office romances, but I believe that it is simply an undeniable fact that while it may not be a morale killer per se, there will inevitably be those workers who carry the attitude that it's nice work if you can get it.

I also came to realize that Chris had a penchant for vocabulary that ran toward the crass and the vulgar. Over the course of the time I worked for him, it became apparent that the lynchpin of his theory of leadership was profanity delivered at high decibels. One thing was clear, he had very little use for anyone who didn't share his view of the world. This view was principally that whatever he says goes, and that the course of events could be made to bend to his liking through the sheer force of his personality. Also, while it was clear that Chris considered himself to be a towering intellect (not to mention a cunning linguist and a master debater), I couldn't help thinking that if he walked in on a book club having a discussion on "Moby Dick," he would think they were talking about a sexually transmitted disease.

The helpdesk manager was a guy named Austin Tayshus. He was the type of person you would want in a position like this, as he was very easy-going and confident in his knowledge and ability to work through technical issues. Many times, when customers called seeking assistance, they would ask for him specifically, even though his job was mainly to manage the workflow and keep everyone engaged. The point is, this guy was good, but there was only so much of him to go around.

As I got more situated in my new position, they decided that I should also learn how to run job tickets through the system to familiarize myself with how the business operates. This is surely a good thing for anyone in a business to know the day to day process, and I figured I would be at it a few days and then happily return to my database sandbox and continue developing an awesome helpdesk program. Unfortunately, a few days into my learning curve on the phones, one of the operators decided to stop showing up for work, so I was pressed into service as a customer service helpdesk operator. At first, about all I could do was listen to calls being worked by those around me and try to wing it as best I could. Days passed, and our missing man continued to be missing. About a week later, we were informed that he would not be returning. I didn't realize it at the time, but this was to be the first of many employee turnover situations that would impact my job.

It took a while, but I gradually achieved at least a semblance of comfort working with the daily grind of the business. I started to notice that the key players in the operation were people who were very much governed by their appetites and habits, a key one being smoking. It seemed that Austin, along with Chris and Marion, had to excuse themselves to the inner sanctum for a cigarette break with alarming frequency. This caused those of us who lacked such an addiction to be thrown to the wolves while they visited in the blue haze of the break room.

I juggled this double duty as best I could, trying to carve out time to hone my skills as a developer, and I started to imagine improved capabilities for the program. One of the things I noticed was that each service call included a field to note the time that the tech was expected to arrive onsite to begin work. I figured that I could add a feature to the main form that if the tech had not called in to report onsite by that time (allowing for time zones), I could display a label on the main screen announcing that fact. I began to regret doing this when Chris started roaming around the back of the room to spot these alerts and would go all J.C. Dithers about it. Sorry for the obscure cultural reference to the Blondie comic strip as the pointy-haired boss from Dilbert might be more appropriate, but the fact is that Chris lacked sufficient hair to go all pointy-haired.

Just about that time, Chris had a falling out with the person who was performing the network admin duties for him, so he decided that I would take over that function. Thus began my career in system administration, highlighted by being trained by the person I would be displacing. At least partially, as Chris brought in an IT consulting business to guide us through the labyrinth of pitfalls and difficulties that we might face. It started to occur to me how inadequate most of my course work at college had been in preparing me for real-world conditions of tech work. Other than my microcomputer database class, which I plunged headlong into with great enthusiasm, the fact is that the degree was called Management Information Systems, and the emphasis was on Business Administration, not Computer Science. In fact, you could get this degree without ever encountering the words computer and science in the same sentence.

One of the guiding principles I adopted from my experience in working with computers is not to be the type of computer nerd that talks down to people I work with. Particularly clients, many of whom do not really have the time or inclination to become conversant with the intricacies of either software or hardware. I guess I have a certain amount of empathy for such people, as I can recall a time when I knew next to nothing about computers. There is an electronics retailer that I have dealt with in the past that exemplified the worst characteristics of this type of behavior. I won't mention this retailer by name, but the letters in this company's name could be rearranged to spell "Bust Bye." I have had some dealings with them that have long since forced me to cease doing business with them or recommend that anyone I know or care about do so. They also gave me the experience of being extremely talked down to, and I did not appreciate it. As a result, I can understand how intimidating it can be for someone who just needs their printer to work or retrieve an email; how they can grow frustrated by the experience, and I have determined not to be that guy.

Another thing one did not do was to make life harder for management, defined as Chris, Marion, or the bookkeeper. We had a young lady, let's call her Laika Dempster Fyre, whose job it was to receive the incoming job requests and enter them into the system so they could enter the workflow queue. Beginning in early January, I started to hear rumblings from Chris due to the fact that jobs were being entered with a start date of January of the previous year, not an uncommon occurrence for anyone who does data entry. Those of you who still write checks are probably familiar with the brain fart of writing last year's date for the first week or two of the new year. Unfortunately, one person's brain fart triggered another person's diarrhea of the mouth, and it was an on-going battle for a few days. A typical exchange went like this:

Chris: "MISS FYRE!"

Miss Fyre: "Yes, sir."

Chris: "Your incompetence at data entry is making it impossible for me to sort job tickets! Please get better!"

Miss Fyre: "I'll try, sir."

Chris: Growl, grumble, stomp back to his desk, say the F-word a lot...

Miss Fyre: (Sob, sniffle).

Finally, one Friday morning around the middle of January, Chris and Marion made their grand entrance about mid-morning as usual, and Chris had decided that enough was enough. He proceeded to pounce on this poor data entry clerk and totally destroy her in full earshot of everyone in the office, and quite likely anyone in other offices on our floor, and possibly even offices above and below our floor. He abruptly ended his tirade with the announcement that she was indeed fired and must leave immediately. It was not a pleasant experience for anyone in the office and, no doubt, worst of all for the person who found herself out of a job. I later heard Chris tell the story of how he came face-to-face with her some months later when she was working at the airport as a TSA agent. I would have given real money to witness that encounter.

Anyway, when the smoke cleared that day, I think that a lot of us in the building had the sense of walking on eggshells. One thing I started to do immediately was to add some code to the program that would look at the entry date. If it was near the beginning of the year, and the previous year had been entered, it would pop up with a few choice words about how anyone could be so careless as to make such a dumb mistake. One guess who the first person was to trigger that message. If you guessed Chris Chan, you would be correct. The other significant development that day was that I became fully aware that I would most likely not be working here when I hit retirement age.

Among the business dealings that the company had going were a couple of contracts that amounted to a massive gravy train. There was a large telecom company in the great white north that engaged us to provide an escort to their remote techs. These guys had to visit fiber-optic bunkers along the trunk lines of their networks and replace network interface cards. These were not the kind of cards that would snap into the slot on a computer motherboard, but large units that were worth upwards of $60,000, so they wanted to make sure the units were recovered after replacement. As cushy a job as this seemed, we still had difficulty with one or two of the contractors we worked with showing up for the assignment, something about getting out in the middle of the night to make it to the meeting place.

Sometime early in the year following my being hired to work directly for the company, we received word that the northern contract would be going south. This caused the tone of things to change drastically at the office. We all got a sense that there would be some fairly significant belt-tightening coming up soon. Also, since the recent changes caused by the 9/11 attacks, the Immigration and Naturalization Service, with whom we had a contract, became the Department of Homeland Security, and we had some changes coming with them as well.

For several months, there were plans to move the office from the third floor of the bank building we were in to a location that would give us greater flexibility and freedom. Chris had a builder doing work on it, and by early February, the new office was ready to move into, and, of course, we chose a Saturday to move the bulk of the equipment and furniture across town. One of the perks that I was excited about was that I would have my own private office, and the servers would be right there with me under lock and key. That is to say, the servers were under lock and key, I was not. Usually. After hauling truckload after truckload of equipment and furnishings, we were ready to arrange desks and computers as we saw fit. The IT consultants worked with us to set up a patch panel for the network and phone system, and we were up and running by Monday morning. Because of the on-call nature of the work, we had to make sure there was no interruption in the availability of phone and Internet so we could manage the service during this time.

Once we settled in, Chris and Marion put their heads together and decided to implement a dress code. Ostensibly, this was to establish that we were coming up in the world and would present ourselves as professionals who took enough pride in our appearance to wear business attire, complete with ties for the men. In reality, it appeared to me that they were making another attempt to target some of the people they felt were not up to company standards, and a really good way to get rid of them would be to force them out of their comfort zone. One guy in particular, who often complained of the quagmire of the helpdesk, lasted about a week without being able to wear jeans to work, and he left. Not long after that, they relaxed the dress code some, to where we could wear khakis and polo shirts with the company logo that Chis had designed and had embroidered on them.

It always seemed to me that Marion was a bit of a queen bee, perhaps as a result of her proximity to the seat of power. She may have overplayed her hand at one point when she insisted that the bookkeeper turn her desk so that Marion could see her computer screen through her office window. That did not go over well, the bookkeeper stating that she felt she did not need to be babysat on her way out the door. A short time later, we had a new bookkeeper.

The first major piece of programming that I did was when Chris told me that he wanted to add a module to the database system that would track consigned parts inventory. A big part of the process of running service calls is keeping track of the replacement parts used on the equipment. Many times, this involves a part being sent by the vendor to perform a covered repair, in which case, they want the old part returned. These parts are usually sent directly to the tech, and then that person is responsible for returning the bad part on completion of the call. Other times, we need to have a way of knowing what is available and how and from where it will be obtained. For example, the contract we had with the banking company to service their ATM units was a fast turn-around job, and so many times the storage location for these was the office of the tech who typically ran these calls. As long as we maintained an adequate network of techs who performed this service, we could make sure they had a modem when they needed it and would return it right away.

Other types of calls needed to have a storage facility that any random tech available could zip over and pick up the part, then document the return via FedEx or UPS and let us know the tracking info. So, it was apparent that having all of this in the database would be a valuable feature, and I dove in to set it up so that our helpdesk workers could tell the tech where parts were and how to get them when they were needed.

One of the key features that the consigned parts system would include in Chris's mind was a system of codes to track the status of parts from arrival at the tech to return of the old part.

He painstakingly crafted a four-step process with a code of A to indicate the part was **At** the tech's location, S to show it had been moved to **Storage**, another S to indicate it was **onSite**, and finally, an S to indicate the old part would be **Sent** back for credit. Thus, the goal was for the part to show a progression of **ASSS**. While I hated to encourage Chris's sophomoric attempt at something resembling humor, I couldn't resist telling him that if he would just make the fourth character a 9, that he would have created a perfectly asinine coding system. From the vacant look he gave me at hearing this, I sort of gathered that he was disappointed in my lack of recognition of his brilliant wit.

Evidently, I developed a confidence in dealing with Chris that I had not experienced elsewhere, in the sense that I was perfectly comfortable expressing myself in, shall we say, more colorful language than it would normally occur to me to use (except for that one time taking class pictures). Once, early in the development of the consigned parts database, Chris discovered that he could go behind the scenes of a form and make some cosmetic changes, and perhaps, got a bit carried away in tweaking the code. Whether this was the cause or not, something became corrupted and triggered a glitch when that module opened. I tracked it down and got it to work, and I told Chris that if he ever opened a form in design mode in our database, that I would reach down his throat and pull his goddam nuts out and would jam them up his rear end so far, they would hang out his frigging nose.[7] I don't think even Popeye would have tried a thing like that, at least not without switching to organic spinach. I meant no disrespect, I just wanted to get his attention.

7   Or words to that effect.

Apparently, it worked, as he grinned sheepishly and agreed that it would be best if he left the programming to the programmer. Still, I have a feeling that few other people in his employ could get away with saying that.

Chris seemed sufficiently impressed with my potential, he told me he was sending me to a seminar on Windows Server Technology that was coming to our town within the next three months. I was eager to participate in this since I figured any training in the technology we were using could be beneficial. What I didn't expect was that he discovered the same training was being offered in a bigger city about 900 miles away later that same month, so he decided to fly me there, so I could hit the ground running. I was skeptical of the need to go to that extent for a two-day seminar, but I decided that it wasn't for me to second guess Chris. I'm sure Marion had a similar perspective since she would probably have rather used the money to go shopping. Who could have blamed her?

The seminar was helpful, but the drawback to me was that it mainly touched on the ways that the administration of Windows 2000 Server differed from Windows NT Server. Having never been a Windows NT Server administrator, I didn't really have a frame of reference that was useful, so I felt some pressure to return home able to be conversant with my new knowledge. The other thing that I would have to deal with was that Chris decided that for him bestowing such a marketable skill, that I should sign a three-year continued employment agreement for the privilege, during which, if I left his employ, I would reimburse him the cost of the training. I wasn't really crazy about the idea, and I'm not sure how enforceable it would have been, but at least I figured it would afford me a measure of job security that was practically unheard of around here.

One week in May of that year, we had a number of key individuals who had simply had enough and left. As I recall, some were of their own volition, and others were invited out. Chris seemed to look for reasons to dismiss employees he felt were acting contrary to his interests, which, in his view, was pretty much everyone at one time or another. One of the modifications to the database I had considered making was a checkbox field named FiredHisAss, but I was sure that Chris's trigger finger would get itchy in a hurry if he had that available to him. We were left with a skeleton crew, and it was all hands on deck for the call center. The same temp agency that sent me over here sent us a lady named Jacquelyn Hyde[8], a recently transplanted New Yorker. From the way she presented herself, it seemed like she would be equally comfortable as a truck driver or a phone-sex operator. At least she could give Chris a run for his money in the crass and vulgar department.

We muddled along for several weeks under this new arrangement of being short-handed and getting new people up to speed or more experienced workers adapting to new roles. Many times, this would involve working straight through what the typical office worker would consider lunch time. To their credit, management recognized the need for everyone to remain at their post

8   Not this person's real name, but the letters in her real name could be rearranged to spell "Hoary Man"

during this time and would usually order in lunch for everyone. One day, we decided against the old standby pizza, tacos, or Subway, and called in an order for burgers and fries to the nearby tavern where we would often go for drinks after work. They were known for their ginormous 1/3 lb. burgers. Keep in mind that this was about the time that people were becoming conscious of the detrimental effects of carbs on healthy eating. I mention this because these burgers featured buns the size of hub caps. As the large, white Styrofoam boxes were distributed to each of us, Jacquelyn opened hers and yelled, "LOOK AT THE SIZE OF THOSE F***ING BUNS!" Just to give you an idea of how my mind works, the instant she said that, the thought that immediately sprang into my head was, 'yes, and if you eat one, that's what you'll be saying in a couple of days when you check yourself out in the mirror, you silly cow.' Knowing me, I would have said that out loud under most circumstances, but given Chris's knack for one-upmanship, I didn't think anyone wanted to go there. So, as painful as it was for me, I had to leave that low-hanging fruit on the branch. I don't know what to tell you, this is just what my life was devolving into at this point.

One of the pitfalls of working in a business that provides round-the-clock support for various types of customers is the constant need to be connected to the office via phone or Internet access. In those days, we had a system of assigning a worker to be on-call during off hours. This was needed because some of our contracts were two-hour response and four-hour completion, such as the ATM service. In those cases, we had arrangements with local techs who would store an extra modem or two at their office/home and be able to run the call as soon as they were notified. When this began, the person who was on-call would carry a laptop with a copy of the database on it and would work the call, then they would transfer the ticket information to the live database when he/she got back to the office the next day. With the help of our consultants, we were able to leverage an early version of the Remote Desktop Protocol, known at the time as Windows Terminal Services, which enabled the on-call person to log in directly to the server, albeit over a dial-up Internet connection, and have access to the live database and run the call in real time. I always thought that the requirement to be one of the techs who worked these calls was a bit onerous since I considered myself a technical person and lacking the people skills needed to be in contact with the public, even if that public was a fellow tech. Plus, I realized that not all techs and business owners were keen on the idea of working at a reduced rate so that we could keep our business viable. As far as Chris was concerned, he was providing a win-win situation for us and the tech, since it was providing marginal revenue that they really didn't have to get out and hustle for. Still, there were those who groused about it.

Some of the customers had another way of looking at the situation. In their mind, it seemed like a good idea to just cut out the middle-man. So they would try to get direct access to the techs that ran these calls, especially as in some locations, it was often the same person each time. They would negotiate a separate arrangement with the tech, and we started to notice the volume of calls dropping over time. As you might imagine, that did not sit well with a type-A person like Chris. So, being on-call made it necessary to not only be knowledgeable about who to call when a job came up in the middle of the night or on a weekend, but also to be savvy enough to not be taken advantage of if a customer called and asked for the phone number of the tech who was going to be coming to the site.

The social aspects of working for this organization were becoming a challenge. Jacquelyn was a particularly difficult person to deal with and was just generally the most unfiltered person I have ever been around. One time, I mentioned my situation growing up with my three brothers who were 13, 18, and 21 years older than I was, and somehow made the observation that two of them were old enough to be my father. Jacquelyn retorted that all of them were old enough, and the thought occurred to me that while that may be true, I was operating from the frame of reference of those who were not raised by wolves and had a unified legal and moral life ethic. After very careful consideration, I decided that the concerns of those who were not raised by wolves and had a unified legal and moral life ethic would perhaps escape the sensibilities of someone of her ilk (it should be noted that whenever you cast someone as part of an ilk, it is never a compliment). Jacquelyn was the type of person who held some strong convictions, one of which is that everyone is entitled to **her** opinion. She would not mince words in expounding on her opinions, such as that she didn't believe in marriage. When I hear someone say that, it makes me think that what they are really saying is that they never learned how to give a crap about anyone but themselves. But that is just my opinion.

As my first year of working in this environment wound down, I had the feeling that I was in a position to grow my skills and contribute as a key member of the team. I could tell it would continue to be a challenge laboring under the constraints of Chris's demeanor, but I had made it this far, and I was up for the challenge.

SECOND-HAND SMOKE

3

BY THE TIME I WAS FINISHING MY FIRST YEAR OF WORKING FOR Chris, I had been involved with computers for about seven years. Maxine and I bought our first computer three years before I went back to college, and in some ways, it served as the impetus for me to continue my education. In those days, dial-up Internet was what most people did using the AOL disks that were ubiquitous at the time. For some reason, I chose to use Compuserve, and one of the features it had was a number of user groups you could join to get information about a wide variety of subjects. One of these groups dealt specifically with Microsoft Access, and some of these users were the real old pros of the system. I developed a rapport with a few of them and got a lot of help early on that was quite possibly more valuable than all of the training I got in college. It seemed one of my talents was the ability to communicate what I needed to be able to do, and then to understand the response. There was a certain member of this group who was especially helpful, a programmer living in England, who took the time repeatedly to write out the code for a function I needed to complete, and with little or no modification, it worked in my application.

During that summer, it became apparent that the helpdesk manager, Austin, was having some trouble at home. He mentioned that his wife had gone through her laundry basket the previous night to find her cleanest dirty thong to put on before she went bar hopping. I guess that would give a person reason to believe they should be concerned about their situation. Apparently, there had been problems for some time, and they were trying to work through them, but not making much headway. Austin decided that they should plan a getaway vacation and try to reconnect. Chris agreed, and since Austin was a key member of the team, he decided to help in any way he could. This help came in the form of a two-week vacation in Hawaii for the unhappy couple, another example of how Chris believed his input could turn a hopeless situation around. So, they went, they enjoyed, they returned, and the following month, they started divorce proceedings. Of course, this added fuel to the fire of Chris's belief that everyone was out to take advantage of him.

Over the next few weeks, Austin went through a period of depression, marked by bouts of lethargy and introspection. He was noticeably less effective on the job, and some of the clients who relied on him to deal with their issues were disappointed, to say the least. There was a period when he could not be relied on to show up for work on time, and on one occasion, Jacquelyn put her foot down and insisted that I drive over to his place and bring him in. I'm not sure where that specifically appeared on my job description, but at the time, I agreed that it had to be done. At one point, Chris made a statement that I felt hit the nail on the head. He told Austin that he felt it was time he let his work interfere with his personal problems. That was a rare moment of Chris exercising just the right amount of irony to get the needed point across, although it is probably unfortunate that he didn't possess the sense of tact that would have him say those things in a private meeting. But I guess, you take what you can get.

The company that Chris was using to assist us with our network technology was going through some tough times, and, in his inimitable way, Chris decided that the best course of action was to buy them out and bring the whole crew on board with us. I saw this situation as adding uncertainty to an already precarious situation. The leader of this group was a guy named Sabastian "Sonny" Beech[9], and he brought with him a collection of geek techs that would feel right at home on "Big Bang Theory." His main network tech, Chip Pyle, was a capable tech, but lacking in people skills (as are most people with computer skills, which is probably why the tech world is attractive to them).

We gradually settled into the new arrangement of staff and the division of duties. Chip made it clear that he considered himself to be the only choice as network administrator, a job that I

9   Not this person's real name, but the letters in his real name could be rearranged to spell "Hurl Blimpy".

neither wanted nor needed. I had plenty to do with developing the helpdesk system and welcomed the assistance of a capable tech to handle the arcane tasks involved in network security. Unfortunately, Chris seemed to think that I was the only one he could trust and was loath to turn over the operation of his servers to this outsider. At one point, Sonny asked me how I would rate my skillset in the network admin role, and I told him that, in reality, I felt that I was the second most clueless person in the company. The whole situation seemed to be a bone of contention with Chip and resulted in me being caught between an irresistible force and an immovable object. I ran afoul of Chip one day when, at Chris's insistence, I changed the admin password on the main server. Chris had the theory that he and he alone should know all passwords and be able to access any employee's workstation and files. No chance of any conflict or friction with the staff there. Well, Chip had a concern (perhaps rightly so) that the admin password is tied to many behind the scenes functions, and changing it would cause certain things to cease to run automatically or unattended. It could also be that Chris's suspicion that Chip was using back doors into the system was equally valid.

Chris was the type of person who had to keep up appearances, and one of the ways he did this was to join a country club. Of course, he had to belong to the hoity-toitiest country club in town. This does not in any way track to his proficiency in golf, it just indicates how certain people occupying a particular socio-economic stratum needed to maintain appearances. So it was that we inevitably had to sally forth to the links for a company golf outing. This club was particularly fussy about anyone breathing their air needed to be properly attired and able to keep up with the players on the course. One of the first questions Chris asked me as the round drew closer was if I could break 100 on a golf round. As my introduction to the game was when my brother gave me his old set of clubs and told me I could figure them out when we were on the course, I was firmly in the high-handicapper camp. I soon realized that breaking 100 would become something of a quest in my search for golf validation. It would not be realized for many years.

The round of golf we played that day did not really establish anyone in our group as a golf wizard. At one point, the marshal came along and told us that there were groups stacking up behind us, and we should skip a hole or two and pick up the pace a bit. By the end of the day, I started to feel extremely intimidated by the fact that there were a large number of expensive houses near the tee boxes that all seemed to have large picture windows on the front. My fear was that these windows were worth more than I made in a few months working for Chris and I wondered if the fact of being here at his behest would in any way shield me from liability if I were to slice a tee shot into one of those windows. I suspected not.

Despite Chris's seemingly benevolent demeanor toward me, I came to be aware that, overall, he had a rather draconian approach to human resource management. He once stated that he intentionally avoided compiling an employee handbook because his attorney advised him that nowhere in the history of business had an employer been able to leverage anything in such a document to their own benefit. Rather, it was always the employee that would use something there against the employer. So, his attitude about putting such a weapon in the hands of someone who was most likely out to take advantage of him was, SCREW THAT! I became concerned about this lack of having things spelled out clearly when I overheard another employee talking about taking a vacation and the number of days available. It seemed that someone would need five years of full-time employment to be able to get two weeks of paid vacation. My attitude toward this situation was very similar to Chris's concerning the handbook.

By mid-Spring, Chip had decided he was not going to be the victor in the clash of wills with Chris, and that Sonny possessed neither the clout nor the motivation to protect him, so he gave notice and quit, on the same day as I recall. A few days later, we started to notice that our mail server was not doing its job and did some investigating. We found that the 'bad mail' folder had filled up to the point that it occupied just about every byte of free space on the hard drive. Even Sonny had to admit that it appeared to be a parting shot from Chip. Nothing like a little Denial of Service attack to say it's been nice working for you. I started to think that Chris was right about people having it in for him, but then I realized that he has a way of bringing it on himself. Still, he had a sense of humor about the situation and bestowed on me the title of Senior Head of Information Technology (you can work that acronym out for yourself). I decided to embrace it to the extent that I specified that I would be the

Data Utilization Manager – Senior Head of Information Technology, and the person at the remote site could be the Director of Internet Programming – Senior Head of Information Technology. It fit with the company culture nicely. It also served to saw my potential critics off at the knees.

It was about this time that Chris decided that he would respect my personal space by issuing the decree that there would be no smoking in his office as long as I had access to it. That was quite a gesture, considering that just about everyone in this company at the time, except for the new bookkeeper, was a smoker. I appreciated the gesture but felt like it was something I would believe when I saw it. It turns out, my suspicions were correct, and this edict, to the best of my recollection, lasted about half a week.

Perhaps one of the things that interrupted the respect for my space was a run-in with a tech in another state who made some disparaging comments to Sonny that got back to Chris about a phone call that he had gotten from "the owner's wife." Apparently, there was a dispute over an invoice, and Marion had gotten into a heated discussion with this tech to clarify how things were when you negotiate a fee schedule with a broker. This tech apparently didn't appreciate being bested by an uppity female, and he made his position known. It wasn't long before this tech was on our 'do not call' list.

I had noticed for some time that Marion did the driving when the two of them drove to the office. I'm not sure when I got a chance to see this for myself, as I was normally one of the first to arrive, and the two of them tended to come in a bit later, and they also stayed later than most. It turns out that Chris had a DUI on his record and had lost his license for a while. After some time, he decided it was time to indulge a whim and buy himself a Hummer, something that was a big thing around that time. It was basically a Jeep on steroids, and the type of people who drove them did so to make a statement. That statement being, "I am attempting to compensate for my feelings of inadequacy by being seen driving a vehicle that could stomp anything you might be driving into the asphalt." Before that could happen, he needed to get his license reinstated. Once that happened, he was soon the proud owner of a luxury SUV that was the envy of all. At least in his mind.

I didn't really begrudge him that indulgence, as I feel that a business owner has the right to enjoy the fruits of their labor. Also, he had obtained more than one SUV as a result of a close working relationship he had with the most prominent car dealer in town (not that I thought he would have a working relationship with any other type of car dealer, but this person was known to be a real piece of work). On a couple of occasions, he tossed me the keys to a Chevy Suburban, and later a Tahoe, and told me to use them to commute to and from the office. I wondered at one point if my neighbors thought I must have joined the Chevy of the Month club.

One of Chris's mannerisms that was particularly galling was his use of word-fillers that people employ when they really don't know what they are trying to say, such as "as it were" and "so to speak." One of his big ones was "if you will," as in, "we went through that toner cartridge like shit through a goose, if you will." I know a lot of people say such things to drive home a point, but Chris always put such emphasis and exaggerated body language into it, that I sometimes wanted to ask him, "well, what if I won't?" While I'm at it, I have to wonder, if I will, what? If I will… take your word for it? If I will… alter my world view to conform to yours? My point is that some people could pull it off and look intentional about it, but Chris was not one of them.

One day, a local business that is a network of support for families in crisis called us and asked if we had anyone who could set up a program for them using the Microsoft Access database system. Obviously, I was intrigued, so we set up a meeting to discuss it. They had another system they had been using for a few years that was built by a developer in a city on the other side of the state. It was becoming difficult to manage as she had some keys built into it that required the purchase of licenses every so often, and they were getting tired of not having access to all of their data consistently. I looked at what they wanted to accomplish, and, while I thought it would be a challenge, I definitely thought I could set up a program that would fill their needs. This would be the first time I had brought any revenue into the company, so it seemed like a feather in my cap. Of course, it would get complicated with the addition of input from Chris.

The person who ran this company, Barb Dwyer[10], explained

10   The letters in her real name could be rearranged to spell "Bramble Sap"

that they were expecting the state to help with paying for the development of the software, but she had found the state stipulated that if any state funds were used for the project, the state would own it outright. This immediately caused the hair on Chris's neck to stand up (I'm speaking figuratively here, as the amount of hair that Chris had from the neck up was minimal), and, being the devoted capitalist that he is, said that would be a deal breaker. He asked if the state bought them a copy of Microsoft Office, did the state believe they owned Office? Barb could see the logic of that argument, as clearly as she could see the futility of trying to explain it to the bureaucrats at the state capital. So, we put discussions on hold while we tried to find a way to resolve the impasse.

A few days later, Barb told us she found a way. They would fund the development of the software through donations to their business, which was a 501(c)3 organization[11]. The amount of cash they could raise this way would not come close to the market value of the program, at least in Chris's mind (and as it turned out, the mind of anyone who develops software to make a living), but he justified it due to the prospect of charging for user support over the life of the system.

I had been working to develop this new family database system for a month or so, and Maxine and I decided we would take a short vacation trip for our wedding anniversary that year. We decided to go to Minneapolis as our baseball team was playing an interleague series there that weekend, and we could do some

11 Meaning a non-profit organization where cash and in-kind giving can get special tax treatment.

shopping at the Mall of America. We had no sooner settled at our hotel when I got a call from Chris saying that he had just fired Austin, the helpdesk manager. This was a major blow, as it seemed to me that Austin was as key a person in the organization as I had ever known. He also stated that the family database people would be ready for me to start loading test data. I said to him, "You realize that I am out of the state at the moment, right?" He said, "Oh, okay, you can start working on that when you get back to the office. And hurry."

The job of setting up the family database turned out to be a welcome distraction from all of the craziness going on at the office. I could concentrate on developing the program and running tests while the service calls were being managed by Marion and Jacquelyn. Barb Dwyer would occasionally call me to request a feature or a report that would be needed that she hadn't thought to mention at the outset, and I came to realize that this is one of the standard operating procedures with clients needing software. Certain key components were glossed over in the proposal phase, only to become vitally important by the time delivery was expected. I was kind of under the gun to get this out the door, so I had to get creative in finding solutions, but it still beat having to work on our service calls. The switchover from their existing program to the one I developed went surprisingly smoothly, and after a few weeks of back and forth between our offices to oversee the process, it was pronounced a success. I even got a hug from Barb, who was extremely happy about all of the time it was saving her people, so I felt like I had accomplished something.

As the year was winding down, Chris and Marion announced that they had joined up with a group of employers who pool their funds to put on a Christmas party with other small companies that wouldn't otherwise have much of an event. It sounded like a good deal as there would be dinner and a show put on by a local group of performers that was very popular. It was a good time with great food and entertainment and, as they say, merriment abounded, *if you will.* And no one *would* more than Chris. Somehow or another, he managed to get himself brought up on stage to be serenaded by the buxom torch singer, and he enjoyed every minute of it. Chris is one of these guys who just naturally makes himself the center of attention, in the sense of someone once describing Teddy Roosevelt as the type who, if he went to a wedding, wanted to be the bride, and if he went to a funeral, he wanted to be the corpse. Well, Chris was being Chris here, and while the singer, who could definitely hold her own, managed to flirtatiously stroke his bald head, Chris, in a move that surprised no one who knew him, got his hands into the act. She handled it graciously, but I have no doubt that she would have liked to do to him what I wanted to do if I caught him groping around in my program code.

Shortly after the start of the new year, we had an all-hands meeting to discuss what everyone knew only too well, that expenses were exceeding revenue. Chris mentioned that he was becoming aware that we had, as he put it, excess capacity in human resources. I got the feeling he was talking about me.

The longer I worked closely with Sonny Beech, I started to realize that I did not enjoy being around him. He seemed to hold the belief that anything I could do for the company was something they could get done much more cheaply and effectively by seeking out a code monkey in India or Pakistan, and that I was little more than an overhead expense. I think the real reason is that he felt that the resources that Chris was devoting to keeping me on the payroll could be used to solidify his own position, which he was beginning to sweat about keeping. I had a particularly nasty session with Sonny that gave me cause to regret that I had signed the agreement with Chris to stay on for three years or have to reimburse him for some training that I had received. It occurred to me that his heavy-handed manner was perhaps the main reason that a number of key techs who had worked for him when we started to use his company's services were no longer with him. I also noticed that Marion was not really speaking to me these days. Whether Sonny had influenced her thinking along these lines, I was never sure, but it seemed to me that staying on here was going to be difficult, to say the least.

I was starting to hear rumors that Chris and Sonny were working on plans to further expand the business. Apparently, there was a company on the other side of the state that was going through some tough times, and Chris had decided that the best way to solve their problems was for him to acquire it, and, through the sheer force of his personality and intellect, return it to profitability. Yeah, that could work. I mean, what better way for a struggling company that had recently taken on another struggling company to prosper, than to take on yet another struggling company? What could possibly go wrong? I started to feel a bit envious of the night watchmen on the Titanic because there was a point in time where at least they had a chance to avert a disaster.

One of the thoughts that sustained me throughout my two and a half years of working for Chris was that, given his volatile temperament, any day a person showed up to work in that office could be their last. And so it was, that one afternoon in late February, Chris drove up to the office in his Hummer, and I was called in to see him and told that he was letting me and half the company go because the business was hemorrhaging cash. I could tell it was particularly hard on him having to let me go along with the person in the remote location as that person had been with him for ten years or more. But business is business, and that was how it laid out. As a gesture of appreciation, he took me to a nearby bar after all the necessary documents were signed off, and we reminisced about the good times. It was a short session that included a phone call from my wife, to who I had to explain where things would go from here. At least I would have if I had the foggiest idea, but there was time to deal with that in the days to come.

One of the difficulties of this was that a few weeks earlier, we had made arrangements to go to Arizona to watch some spring training baseball games and do some site-seeing. It was difficult due to the fact that we had already bought plane tickets, and it was next to impossible to get them refunded. So, we decided to go ahead with the trip, only to curtail some of the site-seeing. We did manage to get to a few games, even got to see Barry Bonds hit a home run. This was about the time it became common knowledge that he had been involved with performance-enhancing substances, and one of his fly balls that was caught on the warning track gave rise to some surly comments from fans in attendance about he should have had another steroid for lunch.

When I got back home, Chris continued to call me in for advice, even insisting that I invoice him as a consultant on a project he needed my help with. The experience I had of working for this organization is one that prompts me to wake up in a cold sweat some nights. I value the experience but vowed that I would never again allow myself to be stuck in a work situation that toxic. Thus ended my pretend job in Chris Chan's make-believe company—if you will. As it were. So to speak. I also came to realize the meaning of AFAHM – A Fool And His Money.

RECOVERY

4

THE ROAD I HAD BEEN TRAVELING FOR THE LAST TWO AND A HALF years had suddenly taken a sharp turn if not a full-blown of-framp. After a while, it became apparent that finding a new job in my chosen field of endeavor would present challenges. Just a week or two after my layoff, I saw an ad for someone to do Web Design for an organization that worked to educate voters about environmental issues. The director of the organization stressed that it was strictly non-partisan, but that members of one political party, in particular, seemed to be more in line with their core beliefs and values. She proceeded to load me up with brochures and posters that touted the philosophical and moral superiority of this party's platform as it related to policies on the environment. I'm not comfortable in a politically charged atmosphere, the furthest I will usually go is to say I may not agree with your bumper sticker, but I'll defend to the death your right to stick it.

One thing that puzzled me was this person pressing to learn about my work history. I had provided a resumé with the highlights of my work history, but she seemed persistent in delving into jobs way further back than I would have thought even the most ardent investigator would need to probe. It occurred to me that she might be trying to use past history as an indicator of my age since she couldn't come right out and ask me that. After very careful consideration, I decided that the stress of working for such a partisan group of non-partisans would not be a great way to have a life free of stress and anxiety, given my aversion to political controversy of any kind, so I politely declined any further discussion of possible employment there.

I was able to keep my hand in programming activities by taking a temp job with the local office of the American Red Cross. This came via the same temp agency that sent me to Chris. They had a system they were trying to use to manage a contact list of first responders to emergencies, and my skillset proved useful. I ended up working for them for a few months until the system was set up so that their volunteers and admin people could run it themselves.

Another opportunity presented itself by the fact that the horse races were coming up, and this time, the photo and video vendor had decided to make the change to a digital system. By now, I had been running the film cameras for 10 years and was considered to be something of an expert on the system. I've always said that there are two qualifications for an expert. An ex is a has-been, and a spurt is a drip under pressure. That is how I felt when they sent me the digital camera, timer setup, and laptop computer and printer a few days before the opening weekend of the races. My orientation on the system was basically them telling me, "here's the equipment, have it figured out by Saturday." With the help of the consultant who worked out of the company's facility at a race track in Ruidoso Downs, New Mexico, I was able to get it working. As always, the bane of my existence on this setup was the connection between the starting gate and the camera that triggered the timer so that the race time would show up on the image. This connection is made by means of a phone wire that runs the length of the track and is tied to a punch panel in the control room. It seems like at this multi-use facility from one year to the next, this line is always getting broken somewhere along the 400 yards or so between the starting gate dock and the crow's nest. Somehow, after a long afternoon of tracking down breaks in the wire and configuring the software in the imaging application, we were ready to run time trials the next day.

At some point during that summer, I learned that the original idea behind the switch to the digital photo system was to have me train the racing stewards to run the system, and then they would eliminate my position. It wasn't a big concern to me as I had been trying to get out of doing this job for years. But it turns out that these stewards are not a tech-savvy bunch, and they were not down with the plan at all. So it looked like I would continue to have job security in this career for quite some time. Fourteen years later, it still does.

As it turned out, my availability to travel to the various tracks on this circuit was opportune, as the guy I had been working with who ran the video system, Phil Matteleven,[12] could not make all of the dates, and I ended up being the video operator while I tried to get the stewards comfortable with the photo-finish system. I went to half a dozen different race tracks that summer and basically ran the video booth so that I could replay races for the stewards when there were objections or evidence of a foul or some other mishap, such as a horse becoming injured or a jockey falling off out of the starting gate. I also set up the photo-finish system so that the stewards could handle it, and I was just a few steps away if, for some reason, they needed to deal with a problem. As long as they managed to capture the horses crossing the finish line, we were good to go.

The other thing that kept me going that year was that Chris, realizing that even though he had full ownership rights to the program that I developed for the network of support for families, he would have no one left in the organization who could support it. So he graciously let me take all of the code and database with me so that I could work directly with the group to continue development and support. All things considered, it was very generous of him, even though the case could be made that it was the right thing to do. But I did genuinely appreciate it, although it would become a source of tension for me down the road. That was partially because Barb Dwyer had political leanings that made me decide when I drove to their office that I should approach from the South, so that I wouldn't have to use my right turn signal, as any display of potential conserva-

12   The letters in his real name could be rearranged to spell "Devil Year."

tive tendencies would be dealt with harshly. One time, I was in the office going over some new reporting requirements that the state would frequently hand down, and she had her Internet browser on a page that contained the latest pronouncement by Pat Robertson, and she pointed at it and said, "that is why I hate Christians!" I forgave her and continued to help out, as I just figured that doing good deeds for next to no compensation was just the Christian thing to do.

Barb retired from the organization not long after that, and the person who became my main contact there was a lady named Helen Highwater.[13] At some point, we settled on a yearly stipend for support and frequent development of new reports, of which there seems to be no end, and help with general questions about how to query the data, which, at this point, has been accumulating for over 15 years.

By the end of the summer, I was starting to come to the discouraging realization that the Access database skills that I had honed so meticulously under Chris's guidance were about as sought after as a dropped bar of soap in a prison shower. After receiving one particularly discouraging rejection letter, I took out my frustration on a small metal filing cabinet in my home office. It didn't work too well after that. Finally, I noticed an ad in the newspaper classifieds that advertised an opening at a local TV station for a Master Control Operator, which is basically a person who runs the on-air switcher for broadcasts of network and local programming. This particular broadcast facility has two stations running out of the same control room, a Fox Network

13   The letters in her real name could be rearranged to spell "Carny Ran Far."

channel and an ABC channel. I figured with my background in video control and also having worked on remote broadcasts for high school sports with my friend Phil, I could probably handle a job like that. Years earlier, when I had a part-time job delivering newspapers along vending machine routes, I would go into motels late at night with their bundles of papers, and I noticed there was always a desk clerk/night auditor who seemed to spend most of the time watching TV. I often thought that would be a great job. I never imagined I might be the person airing the shows they would be watching.

So, I sent an application, and a short time later, I was called in for an interview. There, I met the operations manager, Ross Ewage.[14] He was a weaselly looking guy with no front teeth who made me a little uncomfortable, although he seemed like a nice enough guy. He looked at my resumé and said he thought that I was over-qualified for the job, but if I really wanted it, I could start the day after tomorrow. It wasn't so much a question of wanting this particular job, it was just that I had developed certain habits that I would have found hard to support without a regular income, such as eating hot food and sleeping indoors; plus, the working conditions appealed to me, so I said sure, let's do this. Later, I would become consciously aware that I should never again take a job that is offered during the first interview, because if they are that anxious to have you, it is probably because they are having trouble recruiting and/or retaining workers. Unfortunately, it took a while to figure that out.

---

14   Not this person's real name, but the letters in his real name could be rearranged to spell "Devil's Awl am I."

The schedule that I was put on was somewhat unusual, but I found that it suited me. I would be running the switcher for the ABC side on Friday from 2:00 pm to 10:00 pm, Saturday and Sunday from 10:00 am to 10:00 pm, and then I would run the Fox side on Wednesday 10:00 pm to 6:00 am Thursday. In theory, that would give me 40 hours in four days, and I would have 72 hours off from Sunday night till the following Wednesday. But as they say, in theory, there is no difference between theory and practice, but in practice, there is. It turns out that this station did not do anything much in the way of local origination, such as nightly local news, weather, and sports reports. They had attempted it some months earlier, but the head of the corporation decided it was just too much fuss and bother, so they went back to reruns of "The Simpsons" and "Access Hollywood" during those time slots. So, Ross and the IT guy were informed that if they wanted to keep their jobs, they would be expected to work a shift at the board from time to time. Well, Ross often had things that he would rather do, and so he would ask for volunteers to work his shift on Monday and/or Tuesday. Since there were few takers and I was the new guy, it usually fell to me to take on these extra hours. How hard could it be, right? I mean all you need to do is sit and watch TV for crying out loud.

They hired another guy at the same time as they hired me, let's call him Jack Dupp. Jack's brother Stan (not his real name, but he was a stand-up guy, as opposed to his brother who was, well, jacked up) worked at the station and used to do this job before moving into traffic, which is broadcast lingo for scheduling commercial spots in various time slots. With that kind of pedigree, you would think Jack would be an outstanding operator, and for some reason, he found favor with Ross, who made it a point to give him the best work schedule he could. As things turned out, sitting through one of his shifts could be a challenge, both for the workers, and, no doubt, people at home watching TV.

The work itself was not all that tough. The main thing was to monitor your on-air output and be aware of the schedule of local station breaks so that you could switch in the commercial spot at the appointed time. The syndicated reruns that we would show in the daytime and late-night had a printed schedule of exactly when the break would come, and all one had to do was cue up the commercial spot in the computer and switch the broadcast source. Some shows had two minutes and five seconds of blank space built into them so they would be at the next segment of the show when your spots were done, others just had a few frames of blank tape, which meant we had to stop and recue it when the break was over. It wasn't too demanding, but it was very time sensitive. For live sports, which, in our market, was mostly football and basketball, the network faxed over a format sheet stating at what point in the event there would be a station break, usually preceded by a few network ads and a promo or two, then it was our turn.

For prime time on ABC, we had to record the feed for a one-hour tape-delay on one-inch videotape. We had three hours each evening to record, and the cassettes each held one hour of content. We started recording for most of the first hour on one tape and started a second one about 45 minutes in. After the first tape was running, we would put the second tape on the other tape deck and cue it up so that it could be started after the station break and run seamlessly. Then we continued to record on the first tape until the end of the evening. Oh, I should also mention that we recorded two sets of tapes so that we had a simultaneous backup running if there was a problem with a tape deck or the tape itself broke or was eaten by the machinery (or the dog). The one-inch videotape we had was state-of-the-art at one time, but its time had come. Often, the quality resembled watching TV through a pane of glass that had Vaseline smeared on it.

The overnight shift on the Fox side was a blast. I had done shift work before and didn't really mind staying up all night. The programming was pretty easy, as we had a couple of syndicated sit-coms to start with, and after midnight, the programming shifted to a satellite feed of home shopping network or some guys trying to interest people in collecting coins and stuff. The operators on both sides had a list of shows they needed to record from satellite feeds for broadcast in the coming days. On the Wednesday overnight shift, I also had the task of creating commercial backup tapes so that if there was a problem with the computer, we could toss the tape in and show the commercial, provided we could locate it on the tape. Good luck with that. I'm not sure if they were trying to accommodate the old-timers who were used to throwing tapes to run commercials and were less comfortable with relying on technology to cue up spots, or if it was a lame attempt at CYA on their part. In any event, there were some consequences to missing a scheduled commercial spot, like having to run it for free a few times. We had a set of three eight-hour VHS tapes that would record the entire on-air output of each station, and we kept each one around for a few days so that if there was a question, we could go back and verify that it did play at the required time.

Probably the worst day I had at the station was a Saturday in late October, and a college football game between Michigan and Michigan State went to triple overtime. It was getting to be time for the prime-time lineup to start recording, and it looked like there would barely be time to turn around the start of the run while keeping the recording straight. I could see myself trying to switch tapes about every 10 to 12 minutes. Since we were in the hinterlands of an underutilized time zone, the network didn't see fit to provide us with a special feed of the prime-time lineup for that evening. To make matters worse, the guy running the board on the other side wanted to chat about his day, and it wasn't long before I was hopelessly messed up. Kind of like the old Lucy show where they are trying to keep up with the conveyor belt. Well, at one point, the tape I was recording over suddenly started showing the previous night's sit-com. As if that wasn't bad enough, I later found out that I had missed the message on the squawk box that said the network had decided to provide a separate transmission of prime-time starting with the second hour, so I could have had that clean feed of "Desperate Housewives" that I desperately wanted. Fun times for sure.

During the winter of that year, the station decided to upgrade its capabilities and add a computerized system of recording and playback to replace the tape systems they had been using for years. This was to be a state-of-the-art system upgrade that would propel the station into the late 20th Century era of technological sophistication. Not bad for a station that, in the early 21st Century, had been described by some tech consultants as 'Radio Shack TV.'[15] The company sent their techs to install and integrate the system and train the users. To all appearances, it would give us a great deal of capability to pre-record and store many hours of programming, to the extent that an operator could conceivably record and splice together an entire shift's worth of programs with commercial spots correctly inserted and need only monitor the on-air run to make sure there were no last-minute adjustments needed. This did indeed happen to some extent, but it made some of the operators a bit uncomfortable to think that it may impact their own situation if it became too automatic. They feared that someone could prep the daily schedule in such a way that a single operator could handle both sides of the output. Despite management's assurance that they were nowhere near comfortable with the thought of turning to such a system, it turned out that those fears were well founded.

One of the peculiarities that manifested itself early on was that, given the huge storage capacity of the new server, the station manager, or maybe Ross or the IT guy, decided that a really good use of all this capacity would be to record the station's entire library of recorded episodes of "The Simpsons" onto this new system, thereby ridding them of the need for shelf space for 20 plus years' worth of videotape. The most annoying as-

15   The letters in Radio Shack could be rearranged to spell "Hark! A Disco."

pect of this decision (aside from the fact that they actually considered their Simpsons library to be one of their most prized assets) was that it made a significant dent in the ability to search for shows, commercials, PSAs and etc. There was one big list of recordings that at that time did not have the ability to subdivide into categories, so if you were looking for a Star Trek show you would need to scroll past 17 screens full of Simpsons shows to find what you were looking for.

I realized I was going to have to find a better job before too much longer, even though I was enjoying this one for the most part, except for the feeling that I was being taken advantage of with all of the overtime I was being asked to work. It came in handy, since the job didn't pay nearly what I felt a job with that kind of responsibility warranted. Reliability and attention to detail were necessary and reflected in the quality of our output and was visible to thousands of viewers. Jack Dupp was still being Jack Dupp, and he would forget to record programs, have his audio levels wrong, and would occasionally be AWOL when a station break came up.

On the Friday of Fourth of July weekend that year, I came down with some kind of stomach flu or something that was causing me to barf up some very unpleasant looking substances. I nearly called in and told them I wouldn't be there for a couple of days. But, being it was a holiday weekend, I knew my chances of getting excused for anything short of death were pretty much nil, so I went in. Ross could see that I wasn't feeling well, at least he should have, but his only comment was that I should avoid throwing up on the control board. I managed to comply, but I also determined that I would soon be working elsewhere. As it worked out, I soon was. It was the biggest pleasure I had in a long time when I was able to stop by the station during Ross's shift one evening and give him my two-weeks' notice. By the time I left, I been on the payroll for 10 days short of a year, and in that time, I had put in over 430 hours of overtime.

When I did my exit interview, I got in a little bit of a swipe at Jack and the mentality that kept an individual like him on the crew. I said that the station might find it difficult to retain a vast audience if they continued to rely on half-vast operators.

FINDING A HOME

5

WHILE I WAS BEGINNING TO GET ADEPT WITH USING NEWER METH-
ods to look for work, such as online postings and networking,
I fell back on the old reliable newspaper classifieds to locate
something that looked promising. There was a job posted that
said they were looking for a programmer who was familiar with
Microsoft Access development, and I immediately sent my resumé to them. A few days later, I got a call asking me to come in
for an interview. This business was basically a group of associ-
ates who developed software for computers. I met with a young
lady named Ana Liszt (not this person's real name although the
letters in this person's real name could be rearranged to spell
"Rank in a School"), and she gave me a brief overview of the
company and what the job would entail. She also gave me a
small Access program with a list of code changes to make to it
and asked me to take it home and fix it up per the instructions

and email it back to her. I raced through the assigned tasks in this test and eagerly returned it to her and waited to hear back. Sure enough, a few days later, I got a call asking me to come back to meet with some of the other programmers and certain key people in the organization. One of these, Darrell B. Payne (not this person's real name, but the letters in his real name could be rearranged to spell "Ornery Brat"), turned out to be one of the two partners who owned the company, and I found him to be very amiable and easy-going. We talked briefly about my background in programming, and he asked if I had been told what the position offered in terms of compensation. I told him that it hadn't come up, which was true, and, in fact, I hadn't been overly concerned about it in light of the fact that I was coming from a job that paid just above the minimum wage. I was open to just about any offer (of course I didn't tell him that). He then quoted a figure for a starting salary that was about $4,000 more than I had been making when I worked for Chris a year and a half earlier.

He seemed sufficiently impressed to hand me off to two of the programmers. After sitting with them for a few minutes and hearing them thoroughly rip my code apart that I had handed back from my test exercise, I thanked them and walked out thinking that it was the end of my opportunity with that particular company.

A week or so later, I got yet another call from Ana who told me that they had talked among themselves and were of the opinion that I was well suited to handle the work. They wanted me to come in for yet another interview to meet with some of the department heads with whom I would be working. At this meeting, I was once again to meet with Ana, Darrell, and some other key people, such as Norma Lee Placid[16]. Norma was one of the very early workers in the company and headed up a department that dealt with a program for which this organization did development as well as reselling of the software. One of the questions that came up at this meeting was how soon I could start if I were chosen for the job. As I was still working for the TV station at the time, I said I could start as soon as they needed me to, but that I would like to be able to give adequate notice where I currently worked. That seemed to be the answer that Darrell wanted to hear.

Ana called once more, and I was told that I would be interviewed by the development staff and some of the customer support reps. I went to this meeting prepared to demo some of the software I had written for the family network group. At this interview, I met the lead developer of the document indexing program, Cody Monk, and the user support leader, Skip Church.[17] This interview concluded with Ana telling me that they would be making a decision by the middle of the following week, as they had settled on a choice between one other candidate and me. There was nothing I could do now but wait. On Thursday of the next week, I was sitting home enjoying an actual day off when the phone rang. It was Ana, telling me that they had decided to offer the job to me, and asking if I was still interested. I said, sure. When Maxine got home from work, I let her know that I needed to run over to the TV station to have a little chat with my boss.

16   The letters in this person's real name could be rearranged to spell "Oslo is More."
17   Not these people's real names, but the letters in their real names contain the same number of letters as Cody Monk and Skip Church, respectively.

My first day at the new job was spent getting oriented. I was given the grand tour of everyone I would be working with, many of whom I had met during the interview process. I was told that, initially, I would occupy a cubicle near Ana and the other key players in the department, but that, eventually, I would have my own private office. That was amazing to me, but Ana explained that they believed that software developers should have their own space where they can work without distractions, and since Darrell had considerable skills as a handy-man, he was working on clearing a space for cubicles for other workers, like the support reps, so there would be plenty of office space available soon.

Another key person I met was Fay Kerr.[18] She was married to Joe, the other partner who ran the company, and who, I would learn later, was actually the person who started the whole thing many years ago. Fay did not strike me as the warmest person I have ever met. She just seemed a bit prickly and stand-offish and that you had better mind your Ps and Qs around her. I would come to learn that this was a widely held sentiment. She oversaw HR and bringing new people onboard and showing them the ropes and pointing out that they can park anywhere in the lot except for the spot that was clearly marked as hers. She said that, eventually, I would be given a permit to park in the lot across the street, a road affectionately known as the State Avenue Speedway, as pedestrians would often take their lives in their hands walking across the intersection. Eventually, each month, I would find one of these permits in my box, and I would take that as confirmation that I could look forward to at least another month on the payroll.

18   the letters in this person's real name could be rearranged to spell "Cue in Glumly."

The first few weeks at this new job were spent figuring out what I could do with the program I had been hired to maintain, which tracked elementary and high school students through the daily lunch lines. There were a few rough edges to work through, but for the most part, I was able to handle it. They had one of the programmers that had first interviewed me spend a few days showing me the ins and outs of the code and working through some bug fixes, which I acquitted myself adequately. It is always a challenge when you are working with a program that has had at least three other programmers working on over a span of about three years and only one of them is still working for the company. This was to become a recurring theme of my time with this business.

During my first day or two with the company, while I was waiting for a training session, I was perusing the employee handbook. At least this business felt that it was something worth having, which might be a function of this company spending more on payroll in a year than Chris could generate in revenue in his wildest dreams. I noticed the list of holidays that the company observed. Among them were the day after Thanksgiving and Christmas Eve. This was an extremely pleasant surprise, since I had worked for businesses that did not make a point of showing much concern for employees who might want to spend time with their families and/or a relaxing day off to observe a special day. Some businesses are better suited than others to make this a reality, and I realize that a place like the TV station has to be operational 24/7/365, and so everyone needs to show up for their shift, usually without additional compensation. Then there were employers like Chris Chan, who was a little to the right of Ebenezer Scrooge when it came to employee perks. In fact, while I worked for him, if Christmas fell on a weekend, the only acknowledgment of it was on Friday afternoon saying, "have a nice weekend, see you Monday morning."

After a year of working 32 hours between Friday afternoon and Sunday evening, plus whatever overtime my supervisor decided to send my way, it didn't take long to appreciate the routine of 8-5 Monday through Friday. I got to thinking, gee, this must be how normal people live.

On a lighter note, soon after I started here, they had their company Christmas party, which served to emphasize the importance of connecting the families that were involved with this business. I was able to introduce Maxine to the people I worked with and got to meet a few of the programmers and salespeople who worked out of other locations. One of the traditional customs that they observed was the gift exchange, which featured the ability to steal things. It worked like this. At the beginning of the evening, you would draw a number, and the lowest number drawn could choose a gift from under the Christmas Tree, which had been brought by those participating in the gift exchange. Each subsequent number would have the option of choosing another gift from under the tree, or they could steal another gift that had previously been opened. The person who had their gift stolen could then choose another gift from under the tree or steal another one, the only restriction being that you couldn't steal the gift that had just been stolen from you. This occupied a considerable block of time through the evening and yet managed to finish in time for some good quality entertainment by the local theater group. It was a great time, and I enjoyed the sense of family that was evident with this group of co-workers.

Sometime during the first quarter of the following year, I finally got to move into my new office. It was a spacious office with a view out the window of the downtown bus depot. Years ago, when I worked for the newspaper filling vending machines, it was an area that, while it couldn't be avoided, definitely warranted caution late at night. It wasn't a lot better in daylight. I came to appreciate the solitude and quiet that this placement gave me, along with the ability to hear myself think. I fully supported the company philosophy that programmers should be unencumbered by the need to answer the phone and deal with other distractions, among them, staff meetings. There was not a lot of call for me to attend these meetings, but that meant that there was also less call for me to weigh in on how things should be done. On balance, I figured I was getting a good deal.

At the six-month mark in my employment, I was put through the obligatory performance review. Ana conducted this along with Norma Lee Placid, as I was also doing work for her department, and things went fairly smoothly. At least, there were no glaring defects in my performance they wanted to discuss.

In mid-May of my first full year with the company, I did my usual gig working the horse races down the interstate from home for two weekends. The week following the end of racing,

I started to feel particularly unwell, and by mid-week, I started to notice I wasn't having much call to relieve my bladder. By Friday morning, I had downed my usual two mugs of coffee and still couldn't generate a squirt, so I figured that this needed to be checked on. I was feeling a little cruddy and knew that something was up, so I left the office and drove to the same-day care center of the nearby clinic. When I was brought in to see the doctor, I said the reason I was there was because I couldn't pee, at which the doctor said, "okay, go pee in this cup, and we will try to figure out what is wrong with you." (As Dave Barry is fond of saying, I swear I am not making this up.) "Seriously?" I said, "can we review what we know up to this point?" I did my best to generate anything for the sample and could barely produce a thimble full, so they decided to run a catheter in and see if that would help. Still nothing, so they happily pronounced me free of any need to pee. I told them that it had been nearly a day since my last good squirt, so they decided that my situation warranted a trip through the MRI facility. By this time, I decided to send Maxine a text to let her know what was going on. I figured that would get her attention, as she knew me well enough to know that I typically don't seek medical attention unless there is blood gushing or bones protruding. She showed up while I was in the waiting room after the MRI, and they called us in and announced that I had appendicitis and would need surgery right now. Apparently, the appendix had swollen sufficiently to put pressure on the passage between the kidneys and bladder, and that was why nothing was showing up. Before I went in to have the operation, I called work to let Ana know that I would be out the rest of the day, but she was out, so I left a message in her voicemail. This was the Friday before Memorial Day weekend, so I didn't get to speak with her until the following Tuesday, and her response was, 'So, are you going to be in tomorrow or what?' I guess she wasn't that experienced at managing workers who had to undergo emergency surgery. By Wednesday of that week, I did manage to pull on a pair of sweatpants and a loose-fitting shirt (definitely against policy as stated in the handbook) and drag myself into the office. With the help of painkillers, I got through the next couple of days. While there, I checked the inter-office message system and found that Ana had received my notice of going in for an operation and had sent out a message concerning it. However, it appeared that the only recipient was me (and I already knew). I guess that explained the lack of an outpouring of concern and the absence of any cards, flowers, or candy awaiting me upon my return. Still, I wasn't bitter. Except, maybe, about the candy. This, among other reasons, is why I started to refer to Ana as "Miss Communication."

I slowly recuperated over the next few weeks, and we were introduced to another company tradition, the annual picnic and golf outing. Yes, golf was going to become a big part of this job experience as well. By this time, Maxine had taken an interest in the game to the extent that she was at least willing to tag along and give it a try, mostly for the sake of socializing. We held this event at a much more user-friendly course, and we were placed in the same group as Joe and Fay Kerr. It turned out that Joe was the most avid golfer in the company, and Darrell had originally been dragged kicking and screaming to the course by him.

Eventually, Darrell got the golf bug, and, if anything became even more of an enthusiast about it.

For most of the first year with the company, I was shared between two departments; the one that administered the school lunch Access program, and the one that did the more advanced fund accounting program. I had certain key duties on that program, otherwise, I filled in where I was needed doing bug fixes. I once made the observation that whichever department was having a worse day got me. The time came for me to go through a performance review at the one-year mark. Again, Norma Lee participated in this, at which time, I was told that I would be getting moved permanently to Ana's department to work on our flagship document indexing program. They felt that my skills were sufficient to be able to hold my own there and gradually move away from the school lunch program. As Norma Lee pointed out, we were moving away from being an Access shop, so I needed to concentrate on other areas. At this time, I had been the only guy working in Norma Lee's department, and I referred to myself as the token male there. They gave me a brief send-off, and soon, I was learning the ropes of document indexing and imaging.

For the Christmas party that year, we had a change of venue, but the main features were still there, principally the gift exchange with the option to steal gifts previously opened. When it came to my turn to select a gift, I somehow managed to choose an item that was, shall we say, not safe for work. It was one that one of the notable characters in the company (the letters of whose name could be rearranged to spell "combat yak") chose to contribute. A little uncomfortable, but fortunately, it was quickly stolen from me. I chose not to call the police, instead, I selected another gift from the tree.

During the course of the party, I noticed that Darrell's wife was nowhere to be seen. I guess I didn't think too much of it, neither did I think much of the fact that Darrell and Ana seemed to be paying considerable attention to each other. It wasn't until some months later that I saw a notice in the local newspaper that Darrell was getting divorced. Then it all started to make sense.

Back at work, I was becoming more and more comfortable working with the other programmers, both in my area dealing with my little Access program and with the more robust programs that connected to SQL Server databases. I was a little taken aback by one of the programmers I had been getting some pointers from in the more advanced concepts of the system when she made the comment that Access is not a relational database. I certainly had no illusions about its capabilities in a multi-user setting, as it is not the most robust and scalable system ever, but I also knew that it was very good at being able to define relationships with primary and foreign keys and to enforce them in terms of referential integrity. I mentioned this to one of the Compuserve guys I had corresponded with years ago when I worked for Chris, and he agreed. We decided she must be confusing Access databases with the old, so-called database in Microsoft Works (see the definition of oxymoron). But since I was the FNG[19] here, I decided that this was not a hill I was prepared to die on.

19   Flipping New Guy.

This was the first year that I had any amount of vacation time accumulated, so I decided to take the week of the holidays off and just sit at home and relax. This would become a thing I would make a habit of over the next few years. One thing I did during this vacation was to take a break from shaving. After about 10 days, my beard started to fill out and look not half bad. When I got back to work, a few people noticed right away. One of them was Fay. She initially made some snarky comment about who said it was okay for people to let their beards grow. I thought she was being sarcastic, so I let it pass. A couple of days later, she repeated the comment and came right out and said that the employee manual states that men must be clean-shaven. I was a bit taken aback by this comment, so I decided to see for myself, and try as I might, I could not find that phrase anywhere in the manual. There was a line that said that everyone must maintain a neat appearance, but apparently, if your bias is that beards and a neat appearance are mutually exclusive, then I guess the manual says what you think it says. Of course, there were those around the office with their fair share of facial hair, among them Darrell and several members of the systems admin team, many of whom had been there for a number of years. One day, I was with a group of these people, and Fay stopped by looking for Joe. I muttered under my breath, "there's nobody here but us clean-shaven men." I'm not sure she heard me, but she snorted and walked off.

As I was starting to get used to the idea of having a little bit of disposable income, we started to talk about the possibility of getting a bigger and/or newer house. By now, we had lived in this 1950s basic box-type of house for 15 years, and it was getting to feel a little cramped. So we decided that we would at least see what was available. We started going to the semi-annual 'Cavalcade of Houses' sponsored by the realtors and builders in the area. It was fun seeing modern homes with all the amenities they offered, but it did get a bit depressing seeing the prices being asked for these homes.

That spring, we had the opportunity to take a vacation trip to drive to Omaha, Nebraska to attend a wedding for one of my relatives. This was really the first vacation trip of any length I had taken since I started working for this company. One of the things that appealed to me about the trip was that, in addition to seeing family, I had become aware that in a small town in Kansas there is a museum that is dedicated to the space program. It is an adjunct of the Smithsonian and has an impressive collection of artifacts. So, following the wedding, which included seeing friends from the community where I grew up who had made the trip, we made the journey to Hutchinson to see the Cosmosphere. That place is a space nerd's dream. They have everything from slide rules used by Werner von Braun to the twisted wreckage of some of the early test rockets, and it is one of only three facilities on the planet to have on display an actual flown capsule from each of the Mercury, Gemini, and Apollo programs, including the actual Apollo 13 spacecraft. I could have spent another entire day at this place and may do so again before much longer.

That fall, my 50th birthday came along. I'm not sure if I mentioned it in passing one day, but on that morning, I got in and the door to my office had been shut. When I opened it, I found that my office had been 'decorated' for the occasion. My good friend Skip Church had stayed late and added some special touches to the room, and we all had a pretty good laugh. There were cards and treats and, in general, it was a good day. At the time, it was generally considered that 50 was the new 40. Ten years later, I remember trying to convince myself that 60 was the new 47 or thereabouts. Despite the dire warnings I got in college, it didn't occur to me that my prime time might be running out, but before too much longer, I would be faced with the bitter truth of it.

THE NEW NORMAL

6

BY THIS TIME, MY LIFE WAS SETTLING INTO A ROUTINE OF UNRE-
lenting sameness. I was getting used to the phenomenon of
having weekends off and came to regard it as the spoils of war
in obtaining a bachelor's degree in that I had found a position
that rewarded the achievement of such. My work-day consisted
mainly of designing reports for the new software that resembled
those from the old system, as well as trying to come up with new
ones as they were requested by customers.

One of the new duties I was tasked with was the job of converting
the data in a customer's old system to bring it into ours. Up till this
time, Cody had been performing this necessary function, but he really didn't have the patience with it, since while he was doing that,
he couldn't really continue the development of the actual program,
which was where he was needed. So, I happily adapted myself to this

new duty in the belief that it would become my niche in the group.

Using a few of the smaller programs that Cody had written over the past couple of years, I slowly reverse engineered them to the point that I could make it work, even adapting some of the features with my own new wrinkles that I thought were brilliant, or at least, somewhat clever. It can't be overstated how much Cody helped me in this learning curve. I had been told that he was great to work with, and I found that to be very true. It only took about two months for the code to work well enough to say it was complete, although I was to learn that code is never really complete, it is only good enough to use until you find a way to make it do more.

One thing I had become aware of with Ana was that she thought nothing of being in the office anytime the urge to prove herself overtook her, even on Sundays. Personally, I would rather give up part of a Saturday to take care of some extra work, but not joyfully. I still shudder at the thought of the many hours of Saturday work I put in back in the day with Chris Chan. Not that I am particularly religious about not working on Sunday, but I am a consistent church-goer, although, I have often had to make it conform to my work schedule rather than vice-versa. For the most part, Sunday afternoons are a time to just psyche myself up for the coming week. There was a Sunday afternoon that I recall getting a call from Ana, who was about to send one of the implementation specialists on the road that week for an install that I had worked out the data conversion on, and she said there was a bug in the conversion, and could I run in and fix it right away? Well, I didn't really see much of an alternative, so I drove in and tore into the code to see where the issue was.

This was one of my early data conversion projects, and I was still learning the ins and outs as well as the pitfalls of the process. At this county, the recorder was a guy named Clarence (not his real name, and incidentally, I have noticed that there are very few people under the age of 80 who are named Clarence. If you are a younger person named Clarence, then I'm sorry. Not that I didn't notice you, but that you have to go through life named Clarence). He was a real gem of a guy to work with. Ana would come to me with issues that he had found in going over the converted data, and he often had some passive-aggressive comment that she would find a way to smooth out in relating it to me, lest I take it as criticism of the non-constructive variety and get mad and quit. I'm sure I wouldn't have, but apparently, she didn't want to run the risk of losing her conversion developer along with her school lunch program developer. Anyway, after a while, we all had fond memories of the time we spent working with Clarence.

The neat thing about data conversion is that you are simply moving a record from one database to another, although the records don't always relate the same way in the old system, so you have to identify the key fields and match them up. In the program code, you can stop it at any point and watch the field data move through, so if you know what the expected value is. If it turns out to be something different, you can reason out why it is happening and correct it. This one took a couple of hours to track down, and we were good to go.

We were starting to close in on a suitable house to purchase and had developed a working relationship with a good realtor. We rented a small storage unit so that we could start moving our belongings to it in preparation to make the move. We kept coming back to a house we had first looked at a couple of months earlier and was still on the market. It had just had a price reduction, and suddenly, there was interest in it. We decided to make an offer, but it would be contingent on getting our house sold first. As it turned out, we were not able to get the deal done in time but did manage to find another housed just four doors up the street from that one, so it all worked out.

Moving was a whirlwind of activity, and by the time it was finished, we were worn out. We got friends and relatives to help us haul things, and among the last things to make the trip were the two cats and our 47-gallon aquarium. Over the next few months, we gradually got things organized and could relax and enjoy our nice new home.

The whole Darrell and Ana thing went from getting curiouser and curiouser to seriouser and seriouser, until one day, Darrell sent out an email to everyone saying that he had asked Ana to marry him and, after undoubtedly long and careful deliberation on her part, she said yes. And so, off to Vegas they went with a few key people in the company (I was not one of them) to witness Ana Liszt take Darrell B. Payne as her lawful wedded husband. Thereafter she would be, to all who knew her, Ana L. Payne[20]. Thus, they returned a few days later an old married couple. Well, if not a May-December couple, at least, well, a mid-June

20   I love it when a plan comes together.

to late October or early November couple, anyway. Not that we dwell on such things in this day and age.

On that note, there was a brief time during the evolution of their courtship when I wondered if I was witnessing another example of the gold digger syndrome. It turned out, not really. This situation was different from others I had observed, most notably with Marion DeBos, in that Ana was already a department head when it all started; it had been and would continue to be her core competency. I never heard anyone suggest that they thought it was the case either. Maybe that is a testimony to the generally high regard in which they were held throughout the company, myself included. Even though I give Ana a bad time (because I can), I have a great deal of respect and admiration for both of them.

Things didn't change a lot around the workplace, as this relationship had been going on for quite some time. But from time to time, little things became noticeable. Like Ana deciding to become a vegetarian. I'm not sure what brought that on or if it was about being simply vegetarian or full-on vegan, I was never sure. Now, I have no beef with vegetarians[21], but vegans are definitely a different breed of cat. It seems that with vegans, it is always a political statement, in that they feel the need to display their high-minded sensitivity about not exploiting animals for food or some such hogwash. You have to remember that I was raised on a cattle ranch, and beef is what was for dinner. That is all well and good, and I don't really have an issue with it, except for a couple of observations. One is that mother nature has

21   Rim shot

endowed humans with teeth that are similar to those of dogs or wolves that are designed to tear the leg off of slow-moving ruminates and ungulates and kick them to death with it so they can sit down to a nice tasty meal of carrion. If humans were meant to eat only grains, fruits, and veggies, we would most likely have teeth more suited to the task like those of ruminates or ungulates, perhaps making us vulnerable to the dogs and wolves if not for the fact that we used our God-given intellect to develop firearms. That's all I'm going to say about that. There are other areas that vegans tend to be on their high horse that don't strike me as being consistent with critical thinking, and until they figure that out, they really don't have anything to teach me. End of rant.

As with most businesses, we had a certain amount of staff turnover. One of the people we hired during this time was a lady named Ida Wanda Godare. Actually, when she first came to work here, her name was Ida Wanda Newman, but she got married shortly after joining the company[22]. She started out in customer support and spent a lot of her time product testing and finding issues for us programmers to fix. At that time, there was another guy doing a similar job, and I often felt like the two of them were in a contest to see which of them could find the most obscure bug that needed to be fixed just to give us programmers headaches.

In 2011, Maxine and I were getting ready to celebrate our 20th wedding anniversary. We talked about what we might do, and

22   Neither of these is her real name, but the letters in her real name could be rearranged to spell "ninjas derail me."

since we had discussed several times the possibility of taking a cruise, we thought this would be the ideal time. By now, I had ample vacation time available, so it was only a question of where we wanted to go. I looked at several itineraries and noticed that there were Caribbean cruises that left from Port Canaveral in Florida. This caught my attention because I had always wanted to visit the Kennedy Space Center, and I knew that May 5th of 2011 was the 50th anniversary of the first flight of the Mercury program with Alan Shepard. So, we started to plan our trip around being there on that day, even though our actual anniversary wasn't until the middle of the following month.

In getting ready for this vacation, as with the wedding trip we took a few years earlier, I felt the need to get in shape so that I could wear some of my good clothes as there were formal occasions on the ship, as well as just wanting to look good in general. Maxine was also determined to lose some unwanted pounds and got an early start when she learned of a new diet program that was being touted as a breakthrough in nutrition. It was a program that revolved around consuming powdered protein at each meal for several weeks (the letters in the name of this program could be rearranged to spell "Perdition Ale"), up to a few months if necessary, and she chose to start this right after Thanksgiving. I continued to work at my own fitness regimen, which, in those days, involved getting up early each morning to push myself through the paces of trudging half-hour sessions on my elliptical machine and a few reps of strength training exercises using a lightweight bow flex and a few free-weights. I was making a little progress, but not quite getting where I felt I needed to be. Maxine was having much more success with her program, and I don't think I had ever seen her more dedicated to a diet and fitness program, and the results were becoming evident. She only splurged one time, during the Christmas season, she stopped at Taco John's to have their Nachos Navidad, which is something of a non-negotiable tradition for her at holiday time. A couple of months later, I couldn't deny that she was getting far better results than I was, and I decided to also join the program with about six weeks to go before we sailed.

It was a good thing I did because one of the activities I signed up for on the cruise was an excursion to go parasailing. Of all the activities available, that one appealed to me as it was something I had seen done but never had a chance to try it, and it looked like a blast. The description in the cruise literature said we would be doing a tandem ride, and the fine print mentioned a combined weight limit, which, when I looked at the rate we were dropping pounds on our joint efforts, I calculated that we should just squeak by.

I scheduled two weeks off starting the last week in April, which was when we left on the cruise portion of the trip. We flew to Orlando and spent the night there, and the next morning, we were picked up by Royal Caribbean to be taken to Port Canaveral, about an hour away to meet the ship. We could see the ship, Freedom of the Seas, from quite a distance away, and even from there, it was an impressive sight. As we neared the cruise terminal, the guide on the bus told us that once we boarded the ship, be sure to head directly for the buffet. We appreciated the advice but were also aware that we were still 18 hours away from our parasailing adventure, and we didn't really think we could afford to pack on even an extra pound or two. Not that we really thought they were going to make us weigh in, but you can't be too careful. The night, before we left home, we had carefully packed and tagged our bags with the special tags the cruise line had sent us and could only hope that they would be reunited with us onboard. Then we stepped into the cruise terminal to be herded through the massive facility and gain entry to the ship. The queue that we had to navigate was an enormous maze of ribbons that we moved through with amazing speed, up to the ticket counter where we presented our passports and boarding passes. Here, I will have to apologize for a complete lack of any amusing anecdotes to relate about lost boarding passes or passports accidentally stashed in our checked bags, because we are two of the most anal-retentive travelers you could possibly meet. We just think life is too short to be caught up in mishaps that could be prevented with a little precaution.

Once onboard the ship, we were even more impressed with the size and grandeur of the structure. About 25 years earlier, on a trip to San Diego, I had the opportunity to stand next to the ship that was featured in the TV show "The Love Boat." You could probably fit about three of them in the space occupied by this one, with room left over for the space shuttle, which I could look across the bay and see perched on the launch pad at KSC. Upon locating our cabin, our luggage was waiting for us, along with the tickets for our shore excursions, which we had chosen to arrange far in advance to avoid last-minute snafus. We took a quick look around the ship and finally made our way to the Windjammer Buffet on deck 11. We then worked our way back to the Schooner Bar, where I was to develop a real appreciation for tropical adult beverages based on rum and tequila. There, we were given a brief orientation on what we would be doing the next morning on our first stop at a small private island in the Bahamas, which we were told was only slightly smaller than this ship. Afterward, we went up to the top deck and looked out over the port as we set sail. I felt like the king of the world. One thing I hadn't been prepared for was the sensation of the wind as we got underway. The ship travels at around 22 knots, or approximately 25 mph, and if you happen to be heading into a 20-mph breeze, it is like being in a 45-mph wind, which we dealt with most of the way to the farthest point on our itinerary, Saint Martin. On the return trip, we were traveling with the wind, so it was barely noticeable.

The next morning, we woke up and had breakfast at the Wind-jammer before heading off to the lovely island known as Coco Cay, which is a small island that Royal Caribbean leases from the Bahamian government to use as a private destination for their passengers. Most cruise lines have similar arrangements throughout the region, such as Disney Cruise Lines with their island they call Castaway Cay. To get there, we had to get on a small boat from the ship because there was no pier on this island that would accommodate a ship the size of Freedom of the Seas, so they weren't kidding (much) when they talked about the size of the island in comparison to the ship. We stepped off the boat and were immediately presented with the opportunity to have our pictures taken as a souvenir of this memorable occasion. What the heck. We located the parasailing vendor and were told that they would be heading out momentarily, and we could feel free to look around the area before we left. The moment of truth was at hand. I had been looking forward to this for weeks, and I got the impression that Maxine was a bit apprehensive as she had a little uneasiness, not so much about heights, but motion. We once went on a Star Trek simulation in Las Vegas where you get launched from the Enterprise in a shuttle, and the sensation of motion for her in that was barely overcome by her love of Star Trek. I checked, and there was no scale near the boat dock (I momentarily got an image in my head of the scales they use to weigh jockeys after a horse race), so I figured we were good to go. Once out on the water with two other pairs of eager parasailers, our guides chose us to go first. They cinched us up in the rigging, unfurled the parachute, and let the line out, and we were up, up and away. As we slowly rose to well over 200 feet off the surface of the water, we could look around and see the gigantic ship below us and all the water and beach, and the sensation was exhilarating. Maxine later admitted to being a little hesitant, but at the same time, eager to participate in the experience, and she thoroughly enjoyed it. For a few moments, I felt the most relaxed I had in years. I highly recommend it.

After being reeled in and unhooked from the rigging, the next to go were a pair of young ladies who appeared to be well within the weight limit. They also reported enjoying the experience and said they would highly recommend it. The last pair to go was a couple approaching our age, and the wife was a fun lady to be around, but she was a self-described screamer. She was the most visibly nervous person on the boat at the prospect of being lifted hundreds of feet off the surface by a parachute and hanging out over the ocean (what could possibly go wrong?), and they weren't five feet high when the screaming started. The guides had clearly had experience with this type of tourist before, and on the way back in, they made sure to give them enough of a dip in the water to get their feet wet. "We always do that with the screamers," they said. By the time she was back on the boat, even she was ready to highly recommend the experience to others.

After the parasailing, we took part in a walking tour of the island with a small group of people from the ship. We were told about the history of the local islands and how they had once been the hunting grounds of pirates like Blackbeard. I wouldn't be surprised if there were signs around these islands saying, "Blackbeard slept here," but I don't recall seeing any. We spent the rest of the time available to us on the island taking pictures, having lunch, and enjoying tropical adult beverages based on rum and tequila. If there is a better way to escape the drudgery of a job in the middle of the North American continent, I have yet to find it.

The next day was a full day at sea as we sailed to St. Thomas. I got up early and took a walk on the upper deck around the track they had set up for runners and those who just couldn't quite get up the energy to head to the fitness center to pump serious iron, which was just about everyone on this cruise. At one point,

I saw the screamer lady and her husband who had just got off the flow rider, which is the surf simulator on the aft deck. There were plenty of activities like trivia contests, bingo, and karaoke. I steered clear of karaoke as there isn't enough rum in the Caribbean to get me to do that.

It was a great time, and we would do it again in a heartbeat. When we got back to port following the cruise, we arranged a final shore excursion taking an airboat ride through the glades to view alligators and other wildlife and scenery before being taken back to Orlando so that we could spend a couple of days at Walt Disney World. This was the first week in May, and it turned out to be an excellent time to be there because most schools were still in session, so the parks weren't as crowded as they would be in just a few weeks.

The day we arrived back in Orlando, we were hanging out in the hotel lobby, which was a nice hotel run by a reputable company, and Maxine stopped to chat with a guy in a kiosk near the front desk. She came back to report to me that the nice man there had offered to let us have a couple of passes to the Disney parks if we would do nothing more than attend a presentation the next morning. I was skeptical, but she said she'd had assurance that it would only take 90 minutes, and there was no obligation whatsoever. She was also told that we would be driven to and from this site and would be treated with respect, courtesy, and would cheerfully be handed our passes upon completion of the presentation, no strings attached.

The 'presentation,' which was originally made to sound like it might be a seminar done in a large auditorium turned out to be a kneecap to kneecap sales pitch for a time-share contract. Here's how it played out: we were greeted in the waiting room of this suite of offices by a cheerful, gregarious, and extremely large man with a name badge that said Emerson Bigguns (okay, I admit I don't remember this person's real name, but if that wasn't that, it probably should have been). He started out by asking us how we were enjoying our vacation, then launched into his sales pitch about wouldn't be great to 'own' our future vacations instead of renting them like we were doing now. He continued to tout the benefits of vacation ownership, and, after mentioning a figure that by my quick calculations could most likely comfortably feed and house a family of four, along with a couple of cats and a large dog, for about five years, he could tell that we were not jumping at this opportunity. So, he pulled open a desk drawer and announced that he was going to check his 'inventory' to see if there was anything more modest available. By some miracle, he was able to scrounge up a nifty little package that would likely fit our budgetary constraints. Apparently, he was oblivious to the fact that he had long since maxed out our BS meters, and I was already starting to think of the hours of our lives we were never going to get back from having to sit here at this no strings attached presentation where we would be treated with courtesy, respect, and blah blah blah...

As a last-ditch attempt to talk some sense into us, he involved his manager, who sat down with us and reviewed the offer to see what part of 'owning our vacation' we didn't understand.

We politely, courteously, and respectfully stated that we simply were not in the market for such an opportunity, and could we simply complete the terms of the original offer, which was to get our Disney World passes and get on with the rest of our lives? We were ushered to a small office where a surly clerk seated at a desk whipped out an envelope with the aforementioned passes and sent us on our way. On the way out, I caught a glimpse of Emerson sitting on an overstuffed chair looking beleaguered and dejected. This was a valuable lesson to us about being careful about talking to strangers in kiosks in hotel lobbies, since, in most cases, their entire reason for being there is to separate tourists from their cash.

Having escaped from this presentation with our lives, our fortune, and our sacred honor, plus the Disney World passes, we headed out for an abbreviated day at the Animal Kingdom. One of the first stops was the Jungle Cruise ride. We walked around the park for a while and could see a roller coaster peek out from the top of a hill, and it looked like it wouldn't be too intense, so we decided to check it out. What we didn't realize is that the part you couldn't see took place inside the hill, and it involved coming face-to-face with a yeti (at that moment, I thought of Emerson), and the ride itself reversed course and went backward along the track. It was close to the type of ride where you could toss your cookies at the top and get hit with them when you got to the bottom. From a distance, though, it looked like a mellow ride.

The next day was reserved for Epcot, and it was a blast. Maxine was a little groggy from the experiences of the day before, so I took the shuttle to the park, and she followed when she felt up to it. It gave me some time to check out some things that caught my eye, like a trip to Mars, and a couple of loops around "Spaceship Earth," the inside of the big ball at the center of it all. When Maxine got there, we saw things like a programmed water fountain display and a tour of the global village, where we go to see some cultural displays from around the world.

Our trip to KSC was as good as I had imagined it would be. We got there the day before the big anniversary observance and could tell they were making a big deal of it. There was a gathering area set up for a speaker, which we later found out was Scott Carpenter, the second American in orbit, but we were not able to see him as we had other tours scheduled in advance. The next day, we took the historical tour and actually got to be in the control room from where the Freedom 7 mission was managed 50 years to the day from when it took place and could see a replica of the rocket on the pad.

On our way to the airport for the return trip home, I asked Maxine if we had just had the adventure of a lifetime, or is that what we have been doing the past 20 years? I think the jury may still be out on that one. It remains in my mind, the best vacation I have ever had.

RED SKY AT MORNING

7

ONE OF THE THINGS I LOOK FORWARD TO FROM ONE YEAR TO THE
next is the time when my brother comes to town for a few days,
and we play golf and partake in adult beverages based on rum
and tequila. In the early days of these visits, I still hadn't become all that proficient with golf (in my hands, there was very
little difference between a driver and a lob wedge). But it gave
me a reason to take a few days off work and spend time doing
something better than going to the office, and I enjoyed the opportunity to bond with my brother. When I was a kid, I was seriously bummed when he went off to college and then moved far
away to start a career, as he was the only one I really got along
with. But I think that, even without an education, he was smart
enough to figure out that being far away from that environment
was a good thing. He did introduce me to golf one summer,
and, though it took a while, I finally got fully hooked on the

game. It keeps me sane, but it also keeps me humble. As the saying goes, a bad day golfing is better than a good day working.

A while back, Maxine had been having difficulty sleeping and went in for a sleep study session and was diagnosed with sleep apnea. She had to start sleeping with a CPAP machine, which from my perspective was a little bit like sleeping in the same room with Darth Vader, and that is when it was functioning properly. When it wasn't going so well, such as a pin-hole in the air hose or if the mask didn't seal properly against her face, it could sound like there was a flatulent, asthmatic Wookie in the room. But at least it kept her from snoring. One way or another, it was impacting my ability to sleep some nights, and over the next few months, my struggles to get a full night's sleep would become an issue.

Some time ago, we had hired Huck Foley,[23] a programmer to help with our document indexing program. He was immediately tasked with adding a marriage license module to the program. This new programmer was very much a 'best practices' type of person. He was particularly fussy about securing his data inputs to stave off attacks from the outside, such as 'SQL Injection', which is apparently some sort of performance-enhancing substance for databases[24]. Huck was much more adept at some of the advanced techniques and programming languages that were not common or even possible in the Access programs that I worked in, so I felt a little intimidated, but he was sympathetic and really quite helpful when I came to a point where I needed

23   I've got nothing for this one, sorry.
24   Yes, I know what SQL Injection is, but it is beyond the scope of this book to go into in in any detail. Thank God.

to beef up my conversion utility. He helped me set up a separate module to connect to the database and a system of helper objects to move the data around. This was necessary because we were soon faced with the prospect of having to convert a program that our main competitor distributed, and we thought it would be a real feather in our cap if we could pull this off. Besides the fact that they used Oracle databases for many of their systems, the designer had hit on the idea of using something called a BLOB, which stood for Binary Large Object, a system of storing all of the data for a record in a single field in the database. To make it work in our system, we would need to parse these BLOBs into more standard data and move them around the table structure we had established.

The Dreaded Annual Performance Review

Being the good manager she was, Ana subscribed to the need for submitting to the formality of the annual performance review. At least, having her underlings submit to it, anyway. There are several different forms that this ritual takes. One of the most popular at the time was to have each employee fill out a self-evaluation form, then sit through a meeting with the supervisor to go over how things have gone the past year. Nothing ever gets resolved at these sessions other than to validate that it actually happened. I used to sweat their arrival, feeling like I was going to be pounced on for slacking off, but it didn't go that way. As Ana and others would explain at various times, if anything of a troubling nature needed to be addressed, it would have happened long before this meeting. But I still stressed over it.

Truth be told, I don't think that Ana enjoyed conducting these reviews any more than I did being subjected to them. They were supposed to be done by the end of June so that we would have it done in time for the first paycheck of the new fiscal year to reflect the change in compensation. Ana had a habit of taking a vacation the first part of July, so it could be tight scheduling for these reviews. One year, she didn't get around to it before she left, so she just let me know about the raise and said we would discuss the details at a later time. Weeks went by, and it hadn't happened. About three months later, it was my birthday, and I came in, and Ana sent me a birthday greeting on the internal messaging system and said it was nice of me to come into work on my special day. I replied back and said, "What better way to spend a special day than with the greatest group of co-workers in the best company in the world?" then I said, "by the way, are we ever going to get around to that annual review?" She smilingly said yes, but it never happened. That's okay, there was always next year.

As I mentioned earlier, I was having some difficulty sleeping through the night periodically, and during our weekly developer meetings, my eyes would tend to glaze over. Occasionally, Ana would sit in on them with us so that she could provide the necessary leadership, and, try as I might, I found it difficult not to zone out during these sessions. On one occasion, Huck and Cody got into a discussion on the deep things of behind the scenes data manipulation that, in my sleep deprived state, was like an injection of tryptophan, and my mind felt like clay. Soon after, I was walking by Ana's office, and she called me in and mentioned that I seemed to be falling asleep during our meetings. I wasn't sure which was worse, making her feel like she was boring or making excuses about my difficulty sleeping lately, but I couldn't dispute that falling asleep during meetings is never a good thing. I felt some vindication in the fact that, in the months ahead, I could hear snoring coming from a desk not far from my office.

Shortly after I returned from my big vacation, Huck decided to move on. I was sorry to see him leave as I enjoyed working with him as much as I did with Cody, and I had learned a lot from the time I spent working with him. He was very much into doing things the right way, even if it took a little extra time to develop, thinking that it would save time down the road, and he was a little frustrated with Ana's tendency to want to get projects delivered and do whatever it took to get it working. I certainly fell victim to that methodology, though my programs, in those days, tended to be one-off applications, and I could move on the next one. But the two of them didn't really see eye-to-eye on that issue. The other thing that this programmer objected to was the pay scale was not in keeping with his skill set, and he groused a little about the nominal 'dollar' raises that he was getting. My feeling was that he was definitely worth more. Before he left, he laid the foundation for a system to handle vehicle titles in the document program.

We replaced him with a programmer who had previously worked for a company where I had once considered working. This programmer, Justin Sane[25], seemed to have a personality

25   The letters in his real name could be rearranged to spell "RE: Koala Man."

and sense of humor similar to mine, but he was more outgoing and approachable than I usually was. He could toss around terms like "cardinality," "third normal form," and "software development life cycle," as if they actually meant something. Okay, they do actually mean something, but by this time, I had been trying to fit square pegs into round holes for so long, I was becoming a hard-core cynic. Since by this time, we were running out of office space, he had to occupy a cubicle that was set up just outside the area where Cody and I had our offices.

Shortly after my sixth anniversary with the company, we were called into an all-company meeting where it was revealed that our aforementioned competitor had acquired a company in another state with which we had a reseller arrangement. This was the company that distributed the fund accounting program that I had worked on when I was occasionally helping out with Norma Lee's department. As part of their due-diligence, they made it a practice to visit all the businesses with which their acquisitions had a relationship. Nothing much came of this announcement, it seemed like business as usual, but after they had been to our location and had the grand tour, Ana called a few of us in and said that there is a strong possibility that we would be a target for acquisition by this competitor, the letters of whose name could be rearranged to spell "Loneliest Orgy Tech,"[26] so for the sake of brevity, I will hereafter refer to it as LOT. Since Joe and Darrell had been running this company for some 30 years, they had decided that the time had come for the next big move.

The next few weeks were a daze, with the feeling that things

26   Really.

were about to turn upside down. For my part, there was just a feeling that this company, that seemed like a family, was going to be assimilated by a corporate machine that couldn't possibly understand what it was that made it work. There were numerous meetings and small gatherings over those few weeks to attempt to reassure us that things were great and moving forward as they should. As Darrell once said, it was to ensure the future of the company for those of us who would continue to work there in the coming years, and, after all, did any of us want to face the prospect of working for Fay Kerr? He had a point, but still, there was apprehension. One thing that Joe and Darrell made clear early on was that they would be staying on in a continued employment agreement for up to three years to assist with the transition. I have to admit, it was a generous offer from someone who had just cashed out big-time.

Still, there were those times that seemed a bit melancholy and bittersweet, like the final Christmas party as a company, right up to the final day before the acquisition when there was an office party and get together for drinks at a nice restaurant. Unfortunately, I was unable to make it to that as I had to drive to my hometown for a funeral. I tried not to let that affect my mood at the prospect of returning on Monday to participate in the takeover.

I recall having a gnawing feeling in the pit of my stomach that lasted about four and a half months, until the day that we were visited by the management team of our new headquarters. Even though Spring had just arrived, the feeling I had on my drive to work that morning was very much like what I imagined

Ishmael, a character in a novel I once read,[27] felt when he spoke of "a damp, drizzly November in my soul." We all gathered in the atrium, and Darrell introduced the Executive Vice President, Ollie Gark (not his real name, but the letters in his real name could be rearranged to spell "Blew Dismount"). He noted that the transition occurred on April Fool's Day and hoped we wouldn't regard it as an omen. I still had my concerns. One of the interesting things we got to do in the next few days was to go to some of the clients we had recently brought on with the appeal of replacing this company's systems and telling them that, guess what, they are back giving them the business. I'm glad I wasn't part of those updates.

The Morale Committee

Things weren't all bad during this time. One of the first things that we were introduced to was the concept of morale or team spirit happenings. It had always seemed to me, ever since I had worked here that morale was pretty high, but this new organization felt the need to put a committee in charge of it. The first such happening that I recall was 'Hawaiian shirt day.' As the name suggests, this is where everyone comes to work in casual attire like shorts and, amazingly, Hawaiian shirts. I think it was done after a holiday, so that we were kind of in that mindset anyway. The various offices took pictures of those who participated and wanted to be noticed. I actually wore a shirt from the Caribbean that I got the previous year, but I don't think anybody objected.

27   Moby Dick

Another big event involved a contest to display our artistic ability. We were supposed to draw a picture, and for this contest, the subject was Chewbacca. The email that went out to announce this activity stated that we could do any kind of a drawing we wanted but asked that we limit the time spent on it to 10 minutes. I admit, I am a big Star Wars fan, but it seemed a bit odd to me, so I thought I would have a little fun with them. I googled an ad for Copenhagen and Skoal and drew the tins with the logos as well as I could, and when I handed them in, I said that I misread the email and thought it said to draw chewing tobacco, and by the time I realized my mistake, my 10 minutes was up. They had a chuckle and displayed the drawing with the rest of them (some of which were very good), and some of them even got my joke.

Another big change with the acquisition was the addition of a 'volunteer day' as part of PTO. As it was explained to us, we could take one day off a year with pay to volunteer for a worthy organization as long as we spent the time working with that organization and not sitting at home binge-watching Netflix. That was something that we hadn't experienced before, although I came to find out that many organizations had such a perk.

Then there was the time at Christmas when the committee decided that everyone should decorate their cubicle or office for the holidays. As with the other contests, there was a prize, which was usually a gift card of some sort, and everyone who participated was entered into a draw to get an afternoon off at the company's discretion and convenience. I kept my displays of artwork and personal effects to an absolute minimum, and so my fairly spacious office had very little to attract notice. But here, I saw an opportunity to prove a point, so I placed a small replica of the leg lamp from the movie "A Christmas Story" on the ledge of my window, and let it go at that. The theory being that it was a well-known Christmas themed decoration, so they had to give me credit for participating. When the judges came to check, they didn't think I had done anything, so I just pointed to the window and told them that they at least had to enter me in the draw, but I figured that since it was unlikely that I would ever win a decorating contest of any kind, I would settle for possibly getting an honorable mention for lamest attempt at phoning it in, or something like that. They probably did enter me in the draw, but I didn't win.

During that first year, the management team from the main office made a couple of visits to our location. On one of these visits, they made a particular point of telling us that we would be adopting the agile programming methodology, and we would like it. One of the key features of this model is that time would be broken up into 'sprints' that typically ran two weeks, in which we would group our tasks into logical bits and concentrate on finishing them in some sort of assembly line concept. We would also have to create stories for the purpose behind our tasks and be able to relate to them from an end-user perspective. The most noticeable aspect of this arrangement would be the daily 'stand-up' meetings, which were intended to be a 15-minute get together for the purpose of discussing what we were working on and any difficulties or impediments to our progress and see if anyone in the group had ever had similar problems and how they solved them.

One day, I was walking by Justin's desk, and he mentioned that he had tried to get approval from Ana to take his volunteer day, and she had asked him where he was volunteering. Leave it to Ana to try to ensure that everything was being done 'by the book.' This, apparently, was a concern for him as he told me his plan was to spend the day at home binge-watching Netflix. I told him to just tell her he was volunteering at his local mental health center. He said he could work with that. I was glad I could help.

I was still committed to saving up enough vacation time to take the last week of the year off and sit home and watch college football. I always thought that the week between Christmas and New Year's Day was a great time to take off. Because they gave us paid holidays on Christmas Eve and Christmas Day and New Year's Day, I could get a week and a half off and only have to burn four vacation days. Since this was usually a slow time of the year for our customers as well, I was still able to get this approved with very little difficulty. As for the company Christmas party, things were about to change a bit. In the old days, we had a custom of each employee kicking in about 20 bucks to a fund to buy gifts for Darrell and Joe. I'm guessing that there were additional sources of funding for this because they generally got some nice gifts. In turn, they would give each employee a Christmas card that contained a couple of gift cards, one to Costco and one to a restaurant, like Texas Roadhouse or

Famous Dave's. These typically totaled $100-150 per employee, so it was a good deal for most of us. But now, we were dealing with a huge corporation handing out gifts, so these were on par with a subscription to the "Jelly of the Month Club." A little facetious, I grant you, but they had about as much warmth and sincerity as your typical corporate mission statement.

As we entered a new year, and my situation hadn't really changed that much, I mentioned to Ana that it was apparent to me that this company had a department dedicated to the data conversion work that I had been specializing in for close to five years at this point, so I said I would be open to looking at getting an assignment to this department. She said that it had been discussed, but nothing definite had been decided yet. Besides, they were still trying to determine the future of the school lunch program on which I had been working, and with some of the other detail work on the document indexing application, they wanted to keep my options open. I have to admit that from my perspective, there really wasn't much change in the job description.

We got word, at some point, that there was a big install coming up at the largest county in a neighboring state. Once that was officially signed, there would be a ton of work to do converting the data and images, as there was about 30 years' worth of records to go through. As always, I waited with a mix of apprehension and exhilaration at the prospect of starting to work on such an ambitious project.

As we approached the first anniversary of the acquisition, it was becoming apparent that things were different in our office, as people were changing titles and job assignments (except for me), and, as I began to notice, a few key people had decided to leave. One of these was an implementation specialist I had worked with for a few years; the person that I had thought that Wanda was competing with to find the troublesome bugs in the program so that the programmers would have something to lose sleep over. I was more concerned about his departure than any of the others, as we were working fairly closely to coordinate our conversion utilities and the implementation schedules.

The other big issue I discovered was that Ana said she had spoken with a person who was highly placed in the conversion team and discovered that the standard procedure was that the programmer that developed the conversion program for each county was responsible for running the program on the county's server prior to the implementation team taking the county online. This was a major change in our culture, which was that programmers should be seen and not heard, and only seen to the extent that implementers knew where to track them down to fix any screw-ups that became apparent long before they traveled to the county for the install.

This came into play fairly soon, as I had done one other onsite conversion by the time that Wanda went to a nearby state to run an install. Apparently, everything had gone fine on the day of the live data checkout, which was usually done on Tuesday of the install week so that they could have time verify everything. I was just about to leave work for the day and head home to watch the MLB All-Star game on TV, when Wanda called in a panic and said something needed to be redone on the conversion load. So, I had to spend some time tracking down the issue, work up some code changes, publish the program, and start the onsite conversion again, and then monitor it through the evening from home. It was situations like these that could throw a work-life balance into a tailspin for a while.

ENTER MISS MANAGEMENT

8

THIS IS A TRUE STORY. BEGINNING IN THE MID-1940S AND INTO THE '50s and '60s, the United States government carried out extensive research and development in the field of rocketry and weapons systems, leveraging the skills of the many German rocket scientists that came to us after WWII. One of the early facilities set up to conduct this research was the Jet Propulsion Laboratory in Pasadena, California, where teams of scientists worked to develop the delivery systems for nuclear weapons and to put the first humans in space. This was a time of great fear and paranoia revolving around whether we or the Soviet Union could blow up the world more times than the other. Fortunately, our Germans were better than their Germans, thus ensuring that the forces of goodness and niceness would prevail against the forces of evil and rottenness, or at least that was the ethos of the time. Still, folks needed to relieve the tension, and so at the JPL facility, many of the lovely young secretaries, cooks, and rocket scientists held an annual pageant where they would compete for the title of Miss Guided Missile (insert your double entendre here). Wait, that sounds like I'm saying…, oh, never mind. Anyway, it was all in good fun, and no one took it the least bit seriously, and I'm sure if it were done nowadays that no one would think anything of it.[28]

This is also a true story. It is the story of how I got up close and personal with mismanagement, in the form of Miss Management. I can laugh now about the good old days when I thought of Ana as Miss Communication, but she's married now, and Ms. Communication or Mrs. Communication just didn't have the same ring to it. On the afternoon of day 474 of the LOT regime (a regime is like an ilk that has been weaponized), Ana stopped by my office and told me that the decision had been made to officially transfer me to the data conversion team, which meant that I would be attached to a different regional office and be reporting to a new manager. I seem to recall making some snarky comment to Ana about how I had always hoped that I would have the opportunity to be someone she used to manage, but for the life of me, I can't remember what it was I said. It must have been good because I remember that she said she wasn't sure how to take that, and I said that she could just take it in the spirit in which it was intended.

A few days later, I got a call from this manager, a lady named Talia Wutt (not this person's real name, although the letters in

28   You realize I'm joking about that last part, right?

her real name could be rearranged to spell "Snarl Raw Bitch"[29]). We talked for a while, and though I was determined to give the transfer every opportunity to work out, I couldn't help thinking about the old adage, "be careful what you wish for, because you might get it."

One of the first things that I had to adjust myself to was the daily ritual of the stand-up meeting. As I mentioned earlier, this was a feature of the agile programing construct in which the software developers get together each morning for a 15-minute meeting to discuss what they are working on and any areas with which they may be having difficulty and need advice or assistance. Seems good in principle, but the downside is that you need to have some concept of what you are doing and a way to relate any difficulties in a way that doesn't make you look like a total doofus. Since we had such a far-flung group of developers from various locations around the country, we did this via conference call, so we technically didn't need to be standing, but I asked about this to verify it, just in case. Ana would occasionally walk by my office and look inside during this time and noted that I was indeed sitting at my desk, but I assured her that I was within the guidelines established for our group. For a few days, I called in and just listened to the other programmers in the group. There were a few people whom I formed mental pictures of, that when I finally met them, were a long way from what I had envisioned.

I was told by Talia that, at some point fairly soon, I would need to journey to their office to go through orientation and training.

29   Really.

Even though I had practically invented the process of creating the data conversion programs for the program we developed at our location, I would now need to conform to this group's methods and the tools they used, which made what I had been using look like tinker toys. I could definitely tell that I was going from being a big fish in a small pond to a plankton in a shark tank.

I decided to make this trip the week of Labor Day so that I could come to town with Maxine, and we could have a bit of a getaway and see some baseball games. The team that I followed had a player who was in his final season and was closing in on a base hit milestone. We had made arrangements some weeks earlier to come to town at this time, but a couple of weeks before we were to make the trip, it became apparent that he might achieve this goal while we were in town. The night before we left, he hit two home runs to get within one hit of setting this mark, so it looked like we might be able to see him do it the following night when we had tickets to the game. Unfortunately, that night he went 0 for 4 and was still one hit shy. We decided not to attend the game on Sunday, since in those days, he rarely played on Sundays as it was typically a day game after a night game, and the poor guy was getting along in years and needed a day off once in a while. Unbeknownst to us, however, was that on Monday, the team was scheduled to face a left-handed pitcher, and at this point in his career, this left-handed hitter didn't make much of an impact in that situation. So, he actually did play on Sunday and hit a double to achieve hit number 2500. We went to the game on Monday anyway and got to see them get whooped by their toughest division rival. At this point, we had been going to the games of this team for about 16 years and had witnessed them win exactly one game. I'm amazed they would still sell us tickets.

I came to another disturbing realization while watching this game, I watch way the hell too damn much baseball on TV. We were sitting in the second deck on the third base side, which was our favored location at this ballpark because of its proximity to the club level amenities and concession service. Watching a game on TV, I can usually tell the players via facial recognition without the need to see their number or any identifying info on the uniform. Sitting in this location, I looked down and noticed the home plate umpire in all of his gear, noticed his stocky build and the tuft of white hair sticking down below the back of his cap, and I thought to myself, I wonder if that is Larry Vanover umpiring the plate today. I whipped out my phone and opened the MLB app to bring up this very game, and sure enough, Larry Vanover was listed as the home plate umpire at this location. I would have to admit that the ability to identify an umpire behind his mask and other gear is a strong indication that I need to get a life.

So, that evening, Maxine and I had dinner at the restaurant in the hotel that I was staying in for the week, after which, I took her to the airport so she could head home and go back to work, and I returned to my room to experience a feeling of extreme melancholy. Here I was, on a quest to find my place in an organization I had been with for eight years, and I was having a crisis of confidence. I was not at all sure that this is where I belonged.

The next morning, I got up early and turned on the TV and found the local traffic report. It looked like my worst nightmare of snarled, bumper to bumper traffic. I really learned to appreciate my relatively small town, where we have a rush hour that barely lasts an hour each way, and seldom have anything like accidents that snarl traffic or construction delays that can't be easily worked around. I decided to leave extra early in order to be on time.

One of the perks of the hotel they were putting me up in was access on the next floor up to a 'members only' area where a decent breakfast was provided. As I was filling my plate, I noticed a guy sitting at a table who had the logo of our company on his shirt. This logo is made up of the initials of the company name arranged in such a way that they were said to be 'talking' to each other, but you didn't need to be Chris Chan to think of other things they could be doing. Anyway, I assumed he was the person they had brought in to train me. I walked over to him and introduced myself, and this was indeed my soon to be mentor, Noah Vale.[30] We chatted briefly, and I said I would see him at the office. I finished breakfast and went back to the room to finish psyching myself up for the day ahead.

With the aid of my trusty GPS device, I headed to the office. I still missed the turn and ended up on a totally different freeway headed back to the city, I managed to get turned back on course and arrived at the office. It was a typical professional center located near a half-vacant shopping mall. I went inside and tried to find our suite of offices. I finally arrived and came

30   The letters in his real name could be rearranged to spell "Polyp Racer."

face-to-face with Talia. I have to admit, I was surprised. From talking to her on the phone, I had pictured someone a bit older, but she was about Ana's age it appeared, so I remember having the strong sense that I had been working for a living longer than my boss has been eating solid food.

After the stand-up meeting, Noah and I got down to business. He was a person approaching my age, and we hit it off well from the start. He lived in a small town about as far from where I live as this office is from me. He explained that the company he originally worked for had also been acquired by LOT, and they had an office there at one time, but had closed it down, and now, any of the workers who still lived in that town worked out of their homes. After going through the morning rituals of checking email and updating calendars, we were ready to begin.

He started by giving me an overview of how the software is organized. The big difference between this program and the one I had been working with was the fact that it was built on Java[31], while I had been working exclusively in the Microsoft world. I felt like an Old Testament Bible scholar who had gotten by pretty well for years only understanding Hebrew, but at some point, saw the light and was born-again and realized he was now going to have to learn Greek. Maybe that was overthinking the whole thing, and I'm sure that in Talia's mind, the comparison was more like if you knew how to play the saxophone, you shouldn't have any trouble learning the flute. I'm a little sorry that didn't come up, as it would have been the perfect opening

31   Java is a programming language used by high-end programmers. For some, the leading virtue of this language is that it is "open source." This means, among other things, that there isn't a need to make periodic contributions to the Bill Gates Retirement Fund.

to ask her if she ever attended Band Camp, but the opportunity never presented itself. We went through some of the tools used in the process, and while they differed some from the way I had been operating, I could see some commonality in the process. It still involved taking data in whatever form, whether the actual database or text files that had been exported from it, and moving it into a database that ran our software. So, the objective was the same, only the methods differed somewhat.

Another developer I was to form a close connection with, Xavier Selph[32], was a younger guy who had only been with the company a year or two and seemed to be highly competent. We didn't have much interaction during this week, but eventually, we would be helping each other along as we attempted to make our separate systems coexist.

While I was here, they put one of their crack tech gurus to work assembling a computer that would serve as my development workstation to end all development workstations. At least that was the plan. Since up to that point, I had been exclusively a Microsoft developer, and now had to learn the ropes of the Java environment, the system they put together for me had to accommodate both and be fast enough to keep up with what Noah believed would be a jam-packed process of large data sets and programming tools. By the end of the week, they had this computer ready for me to take home, and I looked forward to firing it up first thing Monday morning. Thus ended my week of hands-on learning, and the only thing I felt I had gained was a sense of having a much better idea of how little I knew about this proprietary soft-

---

32   The letters in his real name could be rearranged to spell "Hoarier Nag."

ware on which I was about to be turned loose. I had been working with the program I knew for so long that I felt I could almost see the ones and zeros moving from one system to the other, but this program seemed to me to be orders of magnitude more complex than anything on which I had worked before.

I returned home and back to my private office with a view across the street of an Art Deco style post office building that looked strangely like a prison wall from this vantage point. I thought of all the things I was going to have to learn over the next few months. It was bad enough having to familiarize myself with a coding language with which I had never been proficient, but doing it with my trainer in another state was daunting, even given the technology of web meetings and video conferencing. Being the old school type that I am, I found that I preferred discussing things face-to-face with someone even though we have highly effective tools for collaboration; the younger workers seem to embrace these tools and thrive with them.

I would learn over the next few months that if there was a one-word description for Talia, it would be 'direct.' Much like above-ground nuclear testing but with less regard for the environmental impact. It first came to my attention when I had just completed a simple image upload for a remote site, and they called to report that they couldn't open any records on the system. Xavier called me to say that we needed to figure out what happened before Talia had a core meltdown. It turned out that I had forgotten to rebuild the database indexes, which, in the environment I had been working in, was not always necessary, but in this environment, always was.[33] A rookie mistake, but Talia had no tolerance for presenting the appearance of being a rookie. It was at this point that I realized that, considering the learning curve I was facing, I could either scale it or explore other career options. Given the state of the job market at the time, it was a daunting decision.

Another thing about Talia that I found very telling was her near obsession with having it known that she was a manager. Many times, she would announce a day or two ahead of time that she would not be able to attend the daily stand-up because she had to go to a 'Managers Meeting' of some sort. I guess she felt that the title validated her in some way.

Among the tools that she employed to 'manage' her staff was a program called JIRA. It is a way of letting teams of workers track their hours, and it creates all kinds of performance metrics. At one point, she hit on the idea of setting up bi-weekly 'sprint review' meetings to discuss our projects and how well we were accomplishing our stated goals. A key feature of these meetings was that we would look at upcoming projects and have to estimate the time it would take us to accomplish each step. The problem I always had with it was that it made the assumption that software development could be tracked like an assembly line process, when, in reality, it often depended on divine inspiration, which is hit and miss at best. The other problem I had with this tool is that it made the sprint review meetings feel like a performance review done in public.

---

33   Again, this is one of those references that may not mean much to the average person, I simply include it to give you an idea of how much it sucked to be me during this time.

Another difficulty I struggled with during this time was the feeling of serving two masters. While I was now a direct report to Talia, who was more than 500 miles away, Ana was the product manager of the program that I was spending most of my time servicing, and her office was two doors down from mine. So, I was constantly at odds with doing things according to the way Talia expected, and getting the results that Ana had grown accustomed to expecting that I could provide. It even got to the point where Talia would prohibit me from attending meetings with Ana to discuss the conversion project I was doing for her product. Needless to say, my frustration and stress levels were off the charts.

One thing I learned to despise was the time tickets that Talia expected us to fill out in JIRA so that she could better manage our time. These were particularly annoying when we had implementers onsite, and it became apparent that there was something wrong with the converted data and images. You would think that with as many iterations of the conversion run as we did onsite for testing, any problems would be identified weeks in advance and patched up with time to spare. This almost never happened. What usually happened was that the second day of the installation, I would get a panicked call from Wanda or one of the other implementers, and there would be something I would have to find in the program and rework for a few records that had issues. Once I identified the issue, I would need to fix the code, re-compile the utility, download it at the site, and re-run at least a part of the conversion. Of course, when Talia got wind of this, she would put a halt to any work being done until a ticket could be created in JIRA so that my time could be tracked against the problem. There were times when it would take more time to create the ticket and post my time to it than it took to do the actual fix. But there was a procedure that must be followed, unlike the good old days, when Ana just expected that the thing that needed to be done was the thing that would be done, and everyone was happy.

Many times, while an implementer was onsite, they would have a run-in with a local network admin or database guru. From time to time, since a few of the implementers we had were women, they would experience some push-back from these techs, who didn't seem to want a woman telling them how to query their databases. I suspect that a fair number of these techs got their jobs by virtue of being a brother-in-law of a county commissioner or some such thing. It certainly wasn't because of their vast knowledge of computer systems. I often thought that if I got a chance to leave this job, I could get on at a county courthouse somewhere, as I wouldn't need to know a freaking thing. I'm sure Wanda felt the same way, and I am equally sure that she had forgotten more about databases than some of the local yokels she met at these places ever knew.

A couple of months later, Talia called me one day to say that she needed me to come to the regional office to train Xavier on the program that I had been developing on for several years. Finally, it looked like I might be able to contribute something. The time she chose for the training meant that I would have to fly there on Easter Sunday, something that would not have been my first choice, but seemed unavoidable. She was also bringing Noah from his home base, and, knowing him, I suspected that the Easter Sunday trip would be even less appealing to him.

In prepping for the week of training, we first had to get Xavier set up with his programming environment, meaning all the licensing and installation of the software he would need. Noah was going to be there to train another programmer in the flagship program, something that I was still trying to master. I remember while I was riding with Noah from the airport, we spent some time discussing the counties we had done work for over the years, and it turned out the Noah also had some dealings with Clarence, the passive-aggressive clerk from the county for which I had done one of my early conversions. The other thing he brought up was singing Talia's praises and telling me that, in his mind, she was the best supervisor he had ever had, in that she really stood up for her team. I was beginning to wonder if we were talking about the same person.

During most of this time, I had been working on a conversion project for a large county, and it was not going all that smoothly. It was a situation where the county had felt some pressure to move to our software, and there was some resistance from the clerk who seemed perfectly happy with what she had been using. Since it was a big project, we made sure to give ourselves plenty of time for development and testing and getting all their data converted. It didn't take long before it took on the look and feel of a major quagmire, both in the user testing of the program itself and with converting the data and images.

In this state, the clerk and recorder's office in each county handled vehicle titles, while in most other states, it is done at the state capitol. This county had over 800,000 titles going back over 40 years or so, and they had been through about three different software systems. Compared to the 18,000 marriage licenses they had, it was apparent what was important to them. Converting all these titles and having them come out in a consistent way was becoming a challenge. But I guess if it was easy, anybody could do it. At least, that is what I kept telling myself to get through the day.

One of the project leaders at the county was a gentleman named Myron[34], and working with him would conjure up memories of Clarence all those years ago. Since there was so much emphasis on titles, he was particularly attuned to that phase of the data conversion, and he was relentless with his examination of the results. One time, he sent an issue report that he had picked up because a glitch in the data involved a title to one of his vehicles. That spurred some quick action in correcting.

During one of the implementation conference calls with the county during User Acceptance Testing (which, in this case, was a bit of an optimistic way to put it), the clerk was being even more combative and disagreeable than usual. She made the comment that using this software compared to the program they had was like going from driving a Hummer to a go-cart. Ana's mood was noticeably subdued for a day or two after that.

As much as I hated to think about it, I realized that it would be

34   Yeah, we'll call him that.

a good idea to get proactive in the business of finding a different job. I knew that I was going to have to get out of this situation, and I was also lucid enough to know that you don't just up and quit a job so you can look for another. I had a few things working against me as I embarked on this quest, one being that while my salary was not exorbitant for my occupation, it was quite a bit above an entry-level position. So I would most likely need to go after a job where I could hit the ground running and be productive with very little orientation and training. I also knew that the question would come up, "why are you leaving your current job considering your salary and benefits?" At least, that is what I imagined would be asked and would need to be answered.

I started my search in the best way I knew how by looking in the newspaper classified ads. This was becoming a hopelessly old fashioned way of doing things, I realized, but it had worked in the past. In an attempt to get with the times, I looked at some online job sites that I had heard were good places to find postings for the type of job I was interested in.

The first interview I got was with a company that handled organizational details for a collection of small businesses. In fact, the company I was with used them for some of their insurance and management needs before the takeover. I responded to an ad they placed stating that they were looking for an Access programmer (sounds familiar already), and I went to meet with the owner and his 'IT guy.' They posed the usual vague and general questions and hypothetical situational issues that could come up in the course of the job. I felt I could most likely handle the position, and they said they would be making a decision soon, it was between just a couple of candidates (also familiar). I left feeling at least a glimmer of hope that there was a chance that this place could be my escape from a bad situation, and over the next few days, I tried not to be too anxious. Well, days turned to weeks, and I finally broke down and called them and spoke to the owner, who said that they had decided to go with the other candidate, and he was just about to sit down and drop me a note to let me know. I guess I could have waited.

FIGHT OR FLIGHT

9

SEVERAL WEEKS HAD PASSED SINCE MY FIRST SERIOUS ATTEMPT TO find a different job had fizzled out. Another opportunity presented itself on one of the websites that I had started following, so I jumped through the necessary hoops and got my application in. Just as I was starting my annual Christmas vacation, they called to let me know that I could come in for an interview. What I liked about it was that it was a job with the college from which I had graduated and was now about a dozen years out. I scheduled the interview for mid-afternoon one day the second week in January. It again bolstered my hopes that all was not lost and that I might be heading toward a positive change in the new year. I had applied for a job with the college as a helpdesk tech shortly after I graduated, but I got the feeling at the time that they were looking for someone who was better educated (I didn't mention this at the interview). When they found out that I had got their Information Systems degree, they mentioned that they were not even offering that degree anymore. Again, time passed with no word, but I did hear on the news that the college was having some challenges with falling enrollment and had to make some cutbacks. Apparently, one of the cutbacks was the person who followed up with job seekers to let them know the status of their application.

The longer my search wore on, the more flexible I got in the type of work I was willing to look at. I even considered retail, and when a large farm and ranch supply store expanded near my home, I made a point of attending their job fair event and filled out an application. Of course, I had the unenviable task of explaining why I was trying to get a job that didn't pay nearly what I was making at that time, and I felt ill-equipped to explain money was not the primary concern for me at the time. Again, it was don't call us, we'll call you. Still waiting to hear back from them.

Eventually, I became aware that there was a local business that did IT outsourcing, and I considered checking them out. I looked at some of the postings they had, and it appeared that they were mostly into the kind of programming that was giving me so many headaches these days. I think the main reason I didn't immediately contact them was that I wanted to keep the possibility open in my mind that this could be an option down the road.

One day, the unthinkable happened. Cody Monk called us into

a meeting and announced that he had accepted a job elsewhere and would be leaving. I could not imagine life around here without him, as he had practically invented our document indexing application. While he didn't express any concerns about the new structure of the company, the fact that he was going to work for a company that made video gambling machines told me that he had pretty much decided that our business model was not what he had in mind.

During this time, Maxine had also been trying to find a different job. She had worked as a bookkeeper for a trade association since 1995. Her boss, Frank Lee Scarlett,[35] was a capable manager, though he could come across as detached and somewhat clueless, and while the job had its perks and benefits, she was having a rough time with a difficult co-worker, whom we'll call Ida Slapter. Some days, it was a tossup who could be more difficult and/or clueless. Maxine was in somewhat the same situation as me; she was more or less painted into a corner by the fact of her longevity with the organization and her specialized knowledge. It was going to be difficult for her to pick up and move to a new situation and get the same pay and benefits.

Maxine would often come home with stories of her frustrations dealing with day to day work issues, many of which involved old dogs and new tricks. She has developed her skills working with productivity applications and is pretty handy with Word documents and spreadsheets. She is no slouch with Access databases, but trying to bring Ida up to speed on these made her head hurt. Something like a simple mail merge seemed beyond

35   The letters in his real name could be rearranged to spell "Barfing Deli Fry."

Ida's comprehension. It made me wonder if Ida had ever tried purchasing a Sunday newspaper from a vending machine.

Then there was the time she had a run in with their traveling sales rep who objected to being on the road too much, so she had to try to accommodate his schedule while, at the same time, keep him as productive as possible. Things came to a head one day when Ida was out of the office and Maxine had to retrieve an email from her inbox, and in the process of doing so, she found an exchange between Ida and the sales rep where they were discussing Maxine's 'control freak' tendencies. Apparently, they had done some online searches to add fuel their belief that Maxine had some severe mental health issues and had discussed this with at least one other employee. It was all that Maxine could do at that point to suppress the urge to quit on the spot. She did call for a meeting with the boss to air out the conflict and decided to stick around, but she became highly motivated to engage her job search immediately.

The main difference in Maxine's experience with job interviews compared to mine was that she does not have a college degree. Being just a few years older than I am, she could sense some reluctance on the part of hiring managers to offer a job to an older worker. With her, all they had to do was say that her lack of a college degree was the difference compared to other applicants. Rarely was her 20-plus years of experience regarded as an asset. Needless to say, she was frustrated. Between the two of us, one couldn't get hired because of no degree, and one of us had education and experience which tended to be seen as over-qualified.

Maxine started to spend considerable time researching job search sites and talking to coaches on the subject. At some point, it usually required spending some money to get the inside scoop on the process of job seeking. I believe that most of these coaches were trying to help, but eventually, she made the decision to stay put.

Other than my near obsession to find a new job, things at the office were going along pretty much as usual. We had the typical challenges with writing data conversions as always, and at one job in particular, I was having some difficulty. This county was one of the few that used an Oracle database in their existing system, and I was finding it difficult to connect to it when I installed my program at their site to run tests. We did a workaround by transferring the data to a SQL Server database and making a backup then loading onto their server. We knew we would eventually need to figure out the connection to run the live transfer, but for testing purposes, this would do. The 'IT Guy' at this site was also the programmer for the existing system, so he felt that he was being bumped from his cushy job being the programming guru for the office, and so we got some static from him at times. Once, when I loaded the current version of the data and asked him to move it to the test environment, it became clear to me that he had replaced it with the previous version. The only way that could have happened was if he deliberately sabotaged my attempt to bring in new data for testing. I called Talia and told her of my suspicions about what had happened, and that I would not put it past this joker to pull such a stunt. She noted my concerns and said to keep at it.

I now had a new sense of urgency with figuring out this Oracle issue, so I tracked down someone at Talia's office who was familiar with that program. After looking at all of the available properties of the database, he noticed a setting in the environment that needed to be updated with each restore of the data, and I was able to connect. I informed Talia of this just as she was ready to throw in the towel and request that the county transfer their old data to a database we could access for purposes of making the conversion. I felt like I had accomplished something good here, and it helped me get through the remainder of the installation.

One of the biggest gatherings I attended while employed here was what was billed as the 'Conversion Summit.' This was where all of the conversion programmers from far and wide would come to the office and spend a week bonding and sharing knowledge with one another. Since the location of this summit was just over 500 miles from where I live, Talia offered me the choice of driving or flying there. I thought about it, and as much as I detest dealing with airports and car rentals, the thought occurred to me that situated between here and there was the county that I had just finished this nightmare conversion. I said that with my luck, my car would break down there, and I would have to spend the night at Myron's house. She thought that was funny, but I had to at least consider the possibility that it might actually happen.

Some of the developers in attendance were the real old pros at this game, and their attitude was that it would amount to a week

of vacation. I wasn't quite there yet. There were some worthwhile training sessions along with some time spent learning how
to work as a team. In one of these sessions, we got to go outside
on the lawn and be blindfolded while one member of the team
who could see clearly tried to guide us in putting together a puz-
zle, much like on Survivor, only with more chance of being hu-
miliated. To that end, Talia followed the group around shooting
a video on her phone and generally making snarky comments.

During this week, one of the most surprising things I heard was
from a developer in this office named Cy Kottick.[36] I had originally pictured him as a much older person, but in actuality,
he could have passed for a more intelligent version of Tommy
Chong. He told us that he had once worked for a large telecom-
munications company that he felt had crushed his soul during
the time he was there. It made me wonder how bad things could
have been there that being here seemed a better option. Still,
Cy had the virtue of being a very knowledgeable, personable
guy who could navigate his way in most any organization he
wanted, while I knew that I was in a position of being neither
indispensable nor promotable.

On the next to the last night of the summit, Talia invited all the
team members directly attached to her office out to eat at a Ko-
rean restaurant. This was the kind of place where you cooked
your own entrees at the table with a built-in flat iron grill. It was
a good time and an opportunity to socialize with people I didn't
get to see face to face that often. I had the sense that Talia en-

---

36   The letters in this person's real name could be rearranged to spell, apropos of nothing,
"A Lonely Jew."

joyed watching all of us backwoods hicks (meaning the old guys) trying to eat with chopsticks. I had experienced this as kind of a younger person elitist thing over 20 years earlier, and I was not about to let it beat me. So, when in Korea, do as the Koreans do. If we were at an Italian place, I could invoke "when in Rome do as the Romans do" and go all Spartacus on them, but then, Spartacus wasn't a Roman, he was a Thracian who was enslaved by his Roman captors, maybe that is what made me think of it. I didn't get around to asking Noah if he thought that was a thing, but I may have to give her the benefit of the doubt.

I was beginning to gain at least a modicum of competence working on the new software. Sometimes this involved a simple addition of some images to the server that they had scanned from old, hand-written documents, and sometimes it was a complete transfer of data from their old system to the new one. I never really got comfortable remoting in to county government servers and working with years' worth of data. It all began to wear on me, and I noticed I was experiencing many sleepless nights. In fact, at one point, I asked Talia when we next had a session to estimate the time involved in the various steps of a project, could I include the time I spent lying awake at night trying to figure out how I was going to get through this group of tasks. I could tell she thought I was kidding, but I knew differently. It was about this time that I realized that I was entering a phase of dealing with ageism and the way it is administered by managers. What Talia wouldn't tell ya is that they don't want to fire anyone for fear of getting hit with a wrongful termination suit. So they embark on a campaign of making life so miserable that a person finally gives up and leaves, making it appear it was their own idea, when the truth was, they had no real choice.

During our meetings, I usually found that Talia was tipping her hand in a manner of speaking, by singling out the 'old guys' for having ideas and practices that didn't conform to the 'millennial way' of doing things. Any mention that I would make of taking some proactive step in heading off difficulties down the road was met with suggestions that I not go down that road, since it was only by following her astute guidance and leadership could we advance as a department. Noah also got more than his fair share of this kind of treatment, even though it seemed to me that he would tend to go off on tangents and ramble on about issues that, even to me, didn't seem like issues, and I could see the rebukes from Talia coming well before she worked up the head of steam. I have sometimes wondered if such episodes altered his opinion of her leadership and management abilities.

It was becoming more and more apparent, all the time, that I needed to get away from this place, and there were times I had to bite my tongue to keep from telling Talia that I have 10 days of PTO and she had two weeks' notice. But I knew before I could do that, I would need to secure other employment, and up till then, my attempts had yielded few prospects. I had considered switching departments and was even beginning to question whether I wanted to continue in software development. It seemed I had just drifted into a job that was not really suited to my abilities and interests. As I'm sure I mentioned to Talia at one time, if I had to interview for the job I was doing at the time, it is highly unlikely that I would get it. She disagreed, and, in fact, still delivered performance reviews that were, on balance, indicative of someone who was more than satisfied with my work. Still, I was neither satisfied nor happy. I recall after an especially rough day of being stuck trying to come up with a fix for an issue that needed to be corrected from a past project, Talia emailed me at the end of the day and wondered how I could have spent all day working on this one thing, and that she would call me in the morning so we could discuss it. I went home that evening and curled up in the fetal position in bed and just zoned out. There were other instances of this happening, and I'm sure it couldn't have been easy on Maxine seeing how the stress of the job was affecting me.

The biggest stress inducer in the situation was the feeling that I was trapped in this mess. Not only was there the fact of having a mortgage to pay, but other expenses were adding up. Also, I saw what the company was paying for our health insurance premium, which for people our age, was just slightly less than the mortgage payment. I did not relish the thought of having to come up with that kind of outlay on my own, but suitable jobs that could provide the necessary income did not seem to be plentiful.

The Bean Counters

I remember seeing an old Far Side cartoon by Gary Larson where an old guy is staring at a chalkboard with a massive equation filling up the board, and in the lower right-hand corner was an equal sign followed by a dollar sign. The caption read, "Einstein discovers that time is actually money." I have often thought to replace the name Einstein with that of any of dozens of managers I have worked with over the years.

One day, I was working on a data migration program, and I got a call from one of the project managers, Cassius King.[37] He was interested to know if I could provide a cost-benefit analysis for writing a program in such a way that it would overcome all of the vicissitudes of the client's data and make it so that it would produce accurate reports without crashing the system. I wasn't sure how I would explain to him my belief that we were supposed to do that all the time. I was really beginning to see the drastic difference between Ana's attempt to be all things to all people and the new normal of being the overhead in the process. In the old days, we would just get the damn thing done and not have to schedule endless meetings to discuss what we should do and how we would do it, and in the process, spend more time than just doing what we already knew needed to be done.

Although I had not yet called Talia "Miss Management" out loud, I caught myself referring to her as "She Who Must be Obeyed," a phrase that I hoped conveyed the contempt I was beginning to feel toward her and her proclivities toward micro-management, at least, in my humble opinion. At one point, she insisted that all of us keep a separate list of the hours we were devoting to various tasks over the course of a week and see how many of them could be classified as 'overhead.' This came up because she felt that some of us were not turning in the kind

37   Get it?

of numbers she expected to see from tasks related directly to our conversion assignments. We had broken them down into steps that, in theory, could be estimated with the precision that an auto repair shop uses to charge for a brake job or a transmission flush. So, given the list of projects we had, anything that added up to normal working hours for a week less the time spent doing our assigned tasks must be slack time, at least the way she figured it. The problem with that theory is that you never know what condition the data you receive is in when you start a project. As I explained to another programmer, usually, the job entails taking data that resembles raw hamburger, or in some cases raw sewage, and making it look good, and wherever possible, to taste good. I had occasion to wonder if some of our clients fully understood the definition of a relational database.

One of the salespeople I worked with in our local office made the observation that he had never seen anything like the capacity of this company to generate meetings. I guess, when you have that many managers, all of whom feel that they have to justify their existence, that is what happens. This salesman had also had some run-ins with Talia, as had others in my immediate area, and it resulted in establishing two distinct groups in our local office:

1. Me

and

2. Those who were glad they were not me.

I'm sure it was becoming apparent to many in the local office that I was under considerable stress and strain, in part because I rarely smiled or joked with people anymore. One person who I felt I could confide in was Skip Church. On more than one occasion when I would walk by his office and the door was open, I would sit down and just vent. He seemed okay with it, if for no other reason than misery loves company. He was getting a lot piled on his plate too, and he admitted to being stressed, though he handled it well. I always thought he was well suited to a management role in the organization, despite the fact that he is basically a decent human being.

It got to the point where Cassius King and a few of the other project managers actually scheduled a weekly conference call to see if we could find ways to squeeze more added value from the time spent on these tasks. I could tell that Noah was definitely other than impressed with these sessions.

Shortly after the beginning of what turned out to be my final year of employment with this organization, Xavier Selph sent an instant message to Noah and me that he needed to have a conference call with us, as he has something he wanted to tell us. What he told us is that he had found another job and would soon be leaving. I was not thrilled at this news, since, for one thing, I really liked the guy, and for another thing, I knew that I would be losing a valuable resource in helping me along with the difficulties of the job. But mostly, I knew it would be more work for me. I think Noah felt the same way.

In fact, not only was Xavier the second member of our immediate team to leave (one had 'transferred' to another department), but also one that management seemed to feel no urgent need to replace anytime soon. So, our group had been reduced in strength by 50%, but there would be no prospect of seeing it brought back to its previous level of capability in the foreseeable future. I had to wonder if it was because of the low work volume, or an inability to interest anyone with the ability to choose to come to work in this department.

The one thing that made my last few months in this job livable was the fact that I had noticed from looking at Talia's calendar that she was going to be taking a three-week vacation during the coming winter and leaving the North American continent to boot. I had long had the feeling that the next best thing to having a vacation myself was the boss going on vacation, not because I wanted to goof off, but because I could work relatively unencumbered by her need to exert leadership. Just knowing that this time was coming up gave me something to look forward to.

When she got back, she said she had decided at a recent 'Managers Meeting' that we would be moving from bi-weekly to weekly sprints. This became the straw that broke the camel's back in my mind, as sprint reviews and the performance metrics they featured were as stressful as anything I had to endure here. I wouldn't be surprised if Xavier would have admitted that these were the reason he sought other employment, as she had raked him over the coals a time or two at these meetings, and I recall him telling me that he felt that she was a difficult person to work for.

Another thing that happened was the continuing ritual of the annual review. These still existed at LOT, even though Talia seemed intent on carrying them out in public during sprint reviews. Even though I had repeatedly been assured that there would not be any surprises, I still felt on edge as the actual ones approached. As before, we were expected to fill out a self-evaluation form and be ready to discuss it with the supervisor. And again, I was pleasantly surprised by the outcome on more than one occasion. I suppose it is possible that a supervisor feels that giving a subordinate an unsatisfactory review can reflect poorly on their own leadership abilities.

What I felt it all boiled down to was that the performance review was just another formality, a hoop to be jumped through. The numbers always seemed to work out to show that I had strengths and weaknesses, and the increase in compensation was pretty much taken for granted, and highly predictable. It could be viewed as the story of an employee who is working just hard enough so they don't get fired for an employer who is providing just enough pay and benefits so they won't (or can't) quit. Or so they thought.

RED SKY AT NIGHT

10

THERE IS A SONG BY A CHRISTIAN SINGER NAMED LAURA STORY called "Blessings" that goes, "'Cause what if Your blessings come through raindrops/What if Your healing comes through tears/What if a thousand sleepless nights are what it takes to know You're near." This song frequently played on the radio as I drove to work, and I found it, for lack of a better word, haunting. I am not hesitant to state the importance of faith in my life, and I feel fortunate that I married someone who, if anything, is even more spiritual and solid in her faith than I am.

When I was going through college as a non-traditional student, I became friends with a guy who was a more typical student type, in the sense that if the school had a football team, he most likely would have been its captain. He was an Accounting Major, and we had several classes together. One Saturday morning, we were sitting in a coffee shop cramming for a Cost Accounting mid-term when he asked me point-blank if I was religious. I always blanch at that term, since my pragmatism causes me to eschew the flakiness and superstition that seems prevalent in the lives of the protestants and evangelicals around whom I live my life. But I told him that, yes, there is a strong spiritual component to my life, so, to answer the question, I would have to say yes. He said, "that's amazing, I never would have guessed that anyone as intelligent as you would be into that." Now, that is a left-handed compliment if I ever heard one[38]. The only response I could give was, "maybe you should think about that." At least I am smart enough to know that I don't know everything, but I know someone who does. That is more than I can say for most of the pseudo-intellectuals I know, who seem to fear that acknowledging a higher power would get in their way of having a funky good time.

My friend Heywood Jablomie has told me that he thinks there are two kinds of people who are big into religion: those who aren't particularly bright, and those who are. Unfortunately, many of the people in the former group are just too lazy to use their God-given brains to reason through the dogma that has been crammed into their heads, and many of those in the latter group figure that they can exploit the others because they know that they will believe any damn thing somebody tells them as long as they sound religious. This is what he likes to call the "Religious Industrial Complex." It is characterized by people who are mainly concerned with showing other people how religious they are. These are the types who would never put a bite of food

38 Not that there is anything wrong with being left-handed.

in their mouths until the man of the house has said a few words over it, who talk the jargon and exhibit symptoms of a neurological disorder when the worship leader takes center stage. In his rather cynical view, they are in it for show. I can't deny that happens, and a well-known religious leader about 2,000 years ago had a few choice words for people like that.

Then again, some of the smartest people I know of have a strong faith-based worldview, and those that some would call simpletons have an inner peace that comes from a willingness to accept a few things on faith. I like to put myself somewhere between these two groups. I may not know how it all came to be, but even if I did, I couldn't do anything about it. I like to say that I lack the faith it requires to be an atheist. But the truth is, I feel that if human intellect is the highest power in the universe, then God help us. In the Bible, we are called on to be a peculiar people, and I know that there are many that abuse the privilege, but one of the things I appreciate about Christianity is that it doesn't discriminate on the basis of credentials, like so many of our institutions do. I was fortunate that my pastor at the time, Reverend Ben E. Diction (not this person's real name, but the letters in his real name could be rearranged to spell "Fob Box") recognized that I was going through some struggles regarding my employment situation, and his support and encouragement got me through some difficult times.

While my faith was a key ingredient in getting me through these times, I have to admit that something else that helped were juice boxes. I mentioned this to Maxine, and she looked puzzled until

I clarified that I was referring to the ones that said Franzia and Vella on them. She said, "oh, you don't mean the single-serving kind," and I told her, "well, some days they are." There were times I just wanted to get a five-liter box of red wine and pull the bag out of it and hook it up to an IV drip (don't try this at home. Only use white wine[39]). This was not a healthy time in my life.

Some of the articles I was reading during this time listed ways to know when it was time to leave a job. Most of these focused on things like no longer caring about the results you were getting or about the people you worked alongside, to the general feeling of dread at the beginning of the week, to the absolute horror of dealing with the boss. I was starting to feel all the above. In fact, I distinctly recall moments when I actually wished I could have a heart attack just so I could take a few days off. I'm sure my doctor would have advised against it, but it showed just how much I hated my life at this point. I started to chalk it up to burnout, which is an even bigger indicator of a problem. I think that burnout comes when you realize that you just were never cut out for the job you find yourself doing in the first place.

Things weren't all that much better for Maxine during this time. She was starting to get results from her job search in the form of interviews. Not all of them were with employers that she would have chosen if she didn't need a job, and some were out of curiosity more than anything. One of them was a tech start-up that did work for the aviation industry, and they were not big on things like paid holidays and vacations, as they felt that

39   No. Really. Don't.

time spent not working was not getting the company anywhere. That sounded to me like another employer with a draconian approach to human resource management.

Not surprisingly, most of her responses to interviews were that another applicant who had a college degree was chosen over her, and that was their out for being able to not chose her based on her age. Just saying.

There is a saying that goes, "it's always darkest before the dawn." As it happened, I was lying in bed one Sunday night and tossed and turned all night without ever getting to sleep. I decided that this constituted a good reason to call in sick on Monday morning. If job-related sleep deprivation isn't an adequate reason to take a sick day, I don't know what is. I just chalked it up to being sick and tired of being sick and tired. Sometime after mid-morning, I got up and switched on my computer and checked out a couple of job sites I had been keeping my eye on, when I saw a posting on one that really jumped out at me. This was from the IT outsourcing company that I had noticed a year or so earlier, and the job they were trying to fill involved something they described as "Electronic Data Interchange." They mentioned that proficiency in Access, Microsoft .NET programming, and SQL Database knowledge would be considered a plus, and I had all three. So, I rapidly fired off my resumé and waited for a response. It wasn't long before I got a call from their recruiter, Colleen Slate[40], who said that it appeared I could be very well suited for this job. One thing the ad stated was that the successful candidate would be working on a one-year contract. I didn't

40   The letters in her real name could be rearranged to spell "An Ear Like Hank."

think much of it at the time because I was focused on the out-come of being the successful candidate, I would finally be able to tell Miss Management that she could take this job and shove it up her boney ass. So, after talking to the recruiter, we agreed on a time for another call with the owner of the outsourcing business to go into detail on my skills and qualifications. I was encouraged by the fact that they did seem interested in vetting candidates in this way, and not snatching up anyone who applied and said they could handle the job. However, a couple of days later, Colleen called me back and said that the owner had decided to trust her judgment about my qualifications and would recommend me for an interview with the client.

This client turned out to be none other than the company that Justin Sane had been working for when he came to work for us. Since then, we had hired another one of their former employees, and he still did contract work for them. I figured I at least had resources that I could tap to get information about them. As I mentioned earlier, this is a company that I had considered applying to soon after I graduated from college. It is a service that manages benefits for employees, that is, they are a third-party administrator for companies that handle their own self-funded benefit plans. At least I was armed with this knowledge when I showed up for the interview.

My interview was scheduled for mid-afternoon one day, and it happened that Noah also had to take the afternoon off, which worked fine for Talia as she had another 'managers meeting' to attend. I only hoped that she wasn't about to implement semi-weekly sprints, so I went to my interview with a heightened sense of purpose. I was interviewed by the IT Department head, who, it turned out, was a different person from the days when Justin worked for this company. The other person at the interview was the head of Apps Dev team, Colt Durkey (not his real name, but I'm sure that the letters in his real name could be rearranged to spell something really sublime or ridiculous if I cared to make the effort), and they told me about the projects going on in the company. The main project being a huge changeover in the software the company was using to process their daily data input. It would involve data conversion and a switch to a web-based interface, which would replace their ancient and clunky command line process. At one point, Colt asked me to describe something in my career history that I regretted. I thought carefully before I said something silly, like working for a company like I currently did, thinking it would raise unwanted questions. So I stated that it was most likely the fact that I waited so long to finish college, but that even at that, I felt that it had helped me to focus and get more out of it than I might have if I had finished when I was younger. He seemed satisfied with the response, and the interview concluded. I left feeling fairly confident that it had gone well, and I had done everything that I could to make a strong case for being hired. I remained as confident and hopeful as I could, and on Friday of that week, I got an email from Colleen who said they had told her that they were down to a choice between one other candidate and me, and they expected to make a decision by Monday. So, I had an anxious weekend waiting to see how it would go.

On Monday afternoon, I heard from Colleen, who said that they were wondering if I would be able and willing to work weekdays from 6:00 AM to 2:30 PM. Considering some of the schedules I had worked over the years, this one did not seem that big a stretch, so I said sure. The main concern that I had was that Maxine and I were getting ready to celebrate our 25th wedding anniversary in just a few weeks, and we had made plans to take a trip out of town for about a week. I didn't want that to be a deal breaker, and I was sure that they would understand that I would need to give at least two weeks' notice at my current company, especially since my division would be down to one programmer, and I would need to transfer as much of my domain knowledge to him as I could, so I was hopeful they would be willing to work with me there. Colleen didn't seem concerned that it would be an issue, so she said she would pass it along. Just before 5:00 that day, she called me back and said that I could start right after the middle of next month, which fit with the time frame I had hoped for.

So, the next morning, I called Miss Management to let her know that I would be leaving, and not surprisingly, she didn't seem to have a problem with it. While she didn't come right out and say that she was perfectly fine with it, I could visualize her giving a fist pump and mouthing the words "mission accomplished." She did think to ask if there was a specific reason why I was leaving, and while I would have loved to tell her that I had no wish to live out the remainder of my productive days under the thumb of a micro-managing bean counter, I simply said that I had felt for some time that this situation was not a good fit for me, and I wanted to explore other opportunities. I told her that I could stay longer than the typical two weeks to bring the team up to speed with my code, but she was sure that two weeks would be more than enough.

Ana and Skip were a bit more visibly shaken by my announcement when I met with them later that morning (Talia would most likely not have approved me attending this meeting had I bothered to tell her I was going). After all, we had been together for more than 10 years at that point, and I'm sure they felt that I was going to be a lifer. Ana even asked me if there was any possibility that I might reconsider. I told her that I felt the decision was final and that Talia seemed more than fine with the idea. Besides, it wasn't like I was ever going to be a manager, or in any other way have anything to say about the direction the company or our department would be heading, other than to answer for all of the time and money we could save by paying attention to overhead and logistics. In fact, I'm a little surprised that Talia didn't offer to come to our office and help me clean out my desk. During the last sprint review meeting that I participated in, Noah Vale expressed some regret that I was leaving, and I said that it seemed to be a widely held sentiment, with one notable exception. That didn't really get a response.

The Friday of my last full week with the company, Ana let me know that my presence was requested at a gathering at a nearby tavern to toast my accomplishments, such as they were, and wish me a fond farewell. Darrell came by and others, such as Cody, stopped by to reminisce about the good old days. The company I would be going to work for was the same company that Justin Sane had come from, and he mentioned a couple of people he knew that I would probably hit it off with. I was a little apprehensive about discussing it with him, as I remembered he said he was not impressed with the company at the time he left. But he said it was mainly about the head of the department at the time, and it sounded like he was no longer there. During this get together, Justin asked me if Talia was the reason I was leaving. Since he had met her and was asking the question, I suspected he already knew the answer, but I said yes, and that I had mixed emotions about it – joy and happiness.

My final day of work for this company was Tuesday of the following week, and one of the HR people at the home office arranged a phone call for an exit interview with me. At this interview, I expressed my belief that this organization had too many chiefs and not enough Indians[41] and that I was maxed out on the abuse I had been getting from this organization. One of my tips to them had to do with the idea that they should accept that they have competent people working for them who actually want to do a good job and just get out of their way. I have no way of knowing if that message ever got back to Talia, and to be honest, I was past the point of caring. Near the end of the day, Talia sent me the obligatory email saying how much she had enjoyed working with me for the past couple of years and wished me luck. I very nearly replied back with a message of congratulations on her win or some such appropriate remark[42] but I thought better of it. At this point, it just didn't seem nec-

41   I know, I know. Cut me some slack, I'm from Squaw Gap, North Dakota for crying out loud.
42   And by appropriate, I mean inappropriate.

essary as I was so glad to be leaving. On the way out, I stopped by Skip's office and couldn't resist invoking Popeye the Sailor, who is fond of saying, "that's alls I can stands, I can't stands no more!" Truer words were never spoken.

Two of the big reasons people stay in a bad situation are the pay and benefits. When I really started feeling trapped was when I saw what it would cost to pay our own health insurance premiums. As it was, going on the COBRA plan was just a few dollars a month less than our mortgage payment. This was in the days of Obamacare when you were required to have insurance or face the consequences. So, I had to make the difficult choice to raid the 401(k) plan that I had been accumulating all these years and put that cash toward paying the health insurance premiums. Fortunately, this was not the only retirement savings plan that I had, but the rep there was reluctant to let me withdraw it for this purpose. I was not quite 59 ½ yet, but since I was over 55, I could do a one-time withdrawal of funds without a tax penalty. I opted for that just to have some cushion.

There are many things that banks and retirement planners don't tell you when they put you into a savings plan. Banks, in particular, are apt to steer you in a direction designed to benefit themselves. There is a well-known financial advisor who has stated that banks will qualify you for about double the mortgage balance you can really afford. Their preference is to keep you in mortgage and car payments throughout your working life; proof of the scripture that says, "the borrower is slave to the lender." If you doubt that, consider the fact that it takes 23 years to pay half of the principal balance on a 30-year mortgage, or that the average car loan runs close to $500 a month for seven years. Is it any wonder that many people feel like they are on a treadmill?

Another axiom that retirement planners use is the "four percent rule" for taking distributions from your retirement savings, meaning you withdraw four percent annually, and, in theory, your savings should last 25 – 30 years. I have never heard anyone say this, but it recently dawned on me that following this plan means that every ten thousand dollars you have in retirement savings nets you about a dollar a day in retirement. That is, four percent of $10,000 is $400, and at a 10% marginal tax rate, it leaves you $360, or about $1 a day for the year. No wonder they call economics the dismal science.

Since I was now going to have close to a month off, I decided to put the time to the best use I possibly could. To that end, I started playing a lot of golf. It had occurred to me that if I would be getting off work at 2:30 in the afternoon, it would be great for golf since I could beat the rush to the golf course and not be rushed to finish before dark. I ended up making significant use of that time and can say now that my handicap plus my age adds up to less than 100. When golfing with a boss or a client, there is value in being able to lose narrowly and look good doing it.

Cats, Cats and More Cats

In my introduction, I mentioned that part of a work-life balance is time spent enjoying the company of loved ones and pets. I have always been fond of cats. I am well aware that there are those individuals who do not share this love of cats. If you are one of these, you might want to skip this section. On the other hand, if you are a good and decent person, you might find it interesting, or at least somewhat amusing.

To many people, pets are one of the great joys of life. Cats, in particular, are said to have a calming influence on their owners, although it can be up for debate as to who is actually the owner in this situation. One of the things we have always noticed about our cats is that they can tell when we are not feeling well and will try to soothe us with their presence.

When I started dating Maxine, she had two cats; a gray short-haired cat named Boots, whose face and paws were white, and a calico cat named Abigale. Boots was a very mellow and friendly kitty, and Abigale was a bit highly strung. It turned out that Abigale had a hyper-thyroid condition, and we had to give her pills for it. I learned about the joys of giving a pill to a temperamental cat. Right after we got married, a friend of Maxine's gave us a kitten from a litter that had been born at their little farm outside of town. This kitten was a gray tabby version of a Maine Coon, and because of her coloring, she reminded me of a cat that I had growing up on the cattle ranch. I had named this cat of mine Pepper, so decided that is what I would name the new kitten. When we brought Pepper home, we found that Boots did not take well to the competition for our attention.

After about six months, she warmed up to the newcomer and learned to enjoy having her around. The two of them would plop themselves down side by side on the kitchen floor and wait patiently for treats to be distributed. We started to refer to them as the 'Bobbsey Twins.'

At some point, a friend of Maxine's moved to town and had to live with her parents for a while and was unable to keep her cat, so she asked us if we would take care of Misty for a while. Years later, we started to refer to Misty as our foster cat. I'm not sure if we had all four of these cats at the same time as we lost Abigale at some point. She went outside one morning when it had started to snow and never did come back. We saw paw prints in the snow on our doorstep, but we never did find out where she ended up. That was kind of a sad time. Still, we had enough of the little critters around that we were getting a reputation for being a bit of a cat house.

Cats are always eager to give back and to show that they care. Often, this takes the form of a mouse carried in and deposited on the floor to show that they are doing their job. One time, Pepper brought a live owl into the house. She came in carrying a small owl that wasn't more than a few weeks old in her teeth. She set it down on the floor, and it flailed around and tried to get away. I was able to usher it outside but got to thinking that it may have been injured. Our veterinarian at the time was known to take in injured raptors and patch them up and release them, so I thought it might be a good idea to take the bird to see him. I found a box to place it in and noticed that it had hobbled over to our next-door neighbor's house and was hiding under a shrub. I rang the doorbell to let them know that I was going to grab the bird, and while I was doing this, their small poodle came charging out and immediately went after the owl. I was able to intervene and pick up the owl and get it in the box and head for the vet's office. At least I was able to take care of this bird's most immediate need, which was to get out of our neighborhood.

In the span of about one year, we had to have both Boots and Pepper put to sleep. It is never a pleasant thing, but it is part of owning pets. Boots was over 18 years old and was just starting to shut down. Our vet told us that considering her age and how well she had been taken care of that if reincarnation was a thing, he wanted to come back as a cat and live at our house. By this time, Misty, our foster cat, was getting along in years, and we thought that she might start getting lonely as we had gone from a three-cat household to just one. We went to the animal shelter and got a cat who I thought looked a lot like Boots. He was a young male cat, and we named him Merlin. He could be a handful, and Misty wasn't so sure that she needed a frisky cat to contend with, but they eventually learned to coexist. Merlin made friends with a cat that another family who lived a couple doors down from us had, and they spent many a care-free day chasing each other up and down trees along our block. When we moved across town, their kids were sad to see Merlin go, and I often wondered if he remembered those times playing with his little friend.

A few months after we moved into our new house, I got up one morning, and Merlin was in the walk-in closet in our bedroom sitting by Misty who was sprawled out on the floor. It almost seemed like Merlin was aware that something was seriously wrong with Misty. We placed her on the bed, but she wasn't responsive, so we took her to the vet who examined her and said it appeared she may have had a stroke and was most likely blind and paralyzed. Without much prospect of her recovery, we had to make the decision to put her down. She had been with us for around 15 years, and Maxine shared the news with her friend who had asked us to take care of her cat way back when.

To ease the blow of losing Misty, we went back to the shelter and looked for a new companion for Merlin. We found a fluffy white cat with a black tail and black markings on his face and ears, and we asked to take a closer look. He was about three years old and very friendly. He seemed to take a liking to us immediately, and we thought he would make a good addition to our household. We decided to sleep on it for a few days, and the following weekend, we went back to see if he was still there. He greeted us when we got there, and it looked like it was meant to be. Since it was Valentine's Day when we officially adopted him, we named him Valentino, or Tino for short. He moved in and made himself right at home, and even Merlin decided he was okay.

Tino was a very sweet cat, although he had a habit of wandering off and not being able to remember how to get home. We got him a tag to put on his collar with his name and phone number and got to meet many of the residents of our subdivision this way. One time, he wandered off and was gone for several days, and we had almost given up on seeing him again, but someone picked him up after seeing the flyers we distributed and brought him home.

When we went on our cruise, we boarded Tino and Merlin at our veterinarian's office. Everyone got along well with Tino, who would jump up on desks and solicit ear scratches and tummy rubs, but Merlin was a different breed of cat when he got near a doctor. They reported having to corner him and throw a blanket over him to be able to handle him at all. They said they all liked Tino so much that they would board him for free, but we had to pay double for Merlin.

When my brother came to see us for his annual visits to play golf, he usually had his small dog with him, and Merlin always got extra fluffy during these visits. In addition to not liking doctors, he really had a problem with a dog encroaching on his turf. Tino didn't seem to mind, as he loved all creatures great and small, but the small ones he tended to eat.

My joy at leaving LOT was tempered a bit in that, during my last full week there, Tino came downstairs just before bedtime early one evening and hopped up on a chair and put his head down. I didn't think too much of it, as he pretty much had the run of the house. The next morning, I got up and did my exercises downstairs as usual and noticed he was still in the chair. This was unusual, as he normally wanted to go outside the first thing in the morning. So, before I left for work, I mentioned to Maxine that he didn't seem to be feeling well, and she may want to see about taking him to the vet. They kept him for a couple of days and couldn't really figure out what was wrong, but he didn't have any pep at all and didn't respond to any kind of treatment. So, they sent him over to another animal hospital and did some tests and figured out that he had pancreatitis, and there really wasn't a viable treatment option. So, we had to make the decision to put him down. That was difficult, as everyone loved Tino.

Since then, Merlin has adapted well to his role as 'only cat' in the house. He has mellowed considerably, but his one non-negotiable is no dogs allowed. The vet's office still appreciates when we schedule his check-ups far enough in advance so that the staff has time to bid for days off.

Changes on the Horizon

Our anniversary celebration was a wonderful time. We were able to get together with friends and family and do things we seldom did. We also realized that a lot can happen in 25 years. Shortly before we got married, Maxine had just started a new job. After about six weeks, they let her go for no apparent reason, and it put a damper on our wedding plans. I had just finished my school picture gig for the year, so my layoff was planned, but with both of us being unemployed, we realized we were headed for an uncertain future. But we decided to put our trust in God to get us through it, and, while it wasn't always easy, we did get through it.

The time off that I got was a welcome time of rest and relaxation, and it would turn out to be all that I would get for some time. I was keenly aware of the fact that I was giving up a lot of vacation time over the next few years, since having worked for the company that became LOT for over ten years, I would be getting five weeks of PTO every year. The problem with that kind of time, aside from the fact the five weeks wouldn't begin to relieve the stress of working for Talia and Ana (mostly Talia), is that by the time you have been with a company long enough to get that much time off, it can be difficult to make use of it, because you are probably in a position of being a key person in the organization and your absence would be felt. There should be people who can cover for you, but it still causes issues, so that by the time you return, there is so much catch-up work to do that it is almost more stressful than just staying there and handling it yourself. When it was all said and done, I had to conclude that if the thing you like most about your work is the time you spend not doing it, it is time to move on.

RHYMES WITH DUCK FAT

11

WORKING FOR A COUPLE OF YEARS AS A CONTRACTOR THROUGH A
staffing agency reminds me of a story I heard once. A guy died
and went to his just reward, and when the Devil met him down
there, he told this guy that he could choose one of three rooms
where he would spend all eternity. He opened the door to the
first room and, inside, he saw a whole bunch of people standing
on their heads on a concrete floor. He wasn't sold on that plan
and wanted to see what else was available.

On opening the door to the second room, he saw even more
people standing on their heads on a wooden floor. It was getting
better, but he still wanted to see the third option.

When he looked through that door, he saw several people who
were on their feet but standing up to their ankles in pig manure,

and they were each drinking a cup of coffee. Despite the smell, the guy decides that this is the most appealing choice and asked to remain there. The Devil bid him welcome to his new home, walked out and closed the door behind him, and just then, this little demon comes gliding up to the group and announces, "Okay everybody, coffee break is over, go back to standing on your heads!"

Lessons Learned in the Contractor Zone

That is what working as a contractor can be like. Here is how it happened for me. Once I realized that I absolutely, positively needed to break away from LOT, I knew I needed something to move to before I could make the change. This was a process that, in reality, took a number of years to implement, because, remember, I was in my late 50s when I really got serious about it. When I finally did make the break, I dove headlong into it without asking too many questions. A few that I maybe should have asked had to do with how life is different for a contractor than for a direct employee. The biggest one turned out to be Paid Time Off. As in, there isn't any. Except for a few major holidays, after you have been on the books for six months or so, you may qualify for the holidays that the staffing agency observes, not necessarily the same ones as the organization for which you are working. But as far as vacation or sick days, those are on you.

The job that I ended up doing through this staffing agency was really nothing like I had done before, even though I had to use similar coding and database management tools. I ended up mostly doing the grunt work that was being done daily so that the programmers who were doing the bulk of software development could concentrate on the task of a massive software changeover and the conversions that requires. I learned the basics of the business and, eventually, I was able to lend a hand in some of the key areas of the change. The head of the operation when I arrived left after about a year, as I think it was all a bit overwhelming for him. A new CIO came on and brought with him several key people with whom he had worked before, and he knew what he could expect from them. Among the new workers that showed up soon after his arrival was a group of workers from India. They came on as contractors and worked a week or two at our location, then they went back to India for a while.

The company that was implementing the change didn't always seem to be able to deliver the desired results on schedule, and there were numerous delays in getting the software to perform up to the standards we required. They no doubt had workers from India helping them, but our Indians were better than their Indians[43], and so we finally got the system up and running.

I had an experience early in my time with this company that tempered my enthusiasm toward it to some extent. The job I was doing was highly task-oriented, and most of it was time-critical, so other departments could carry out their functions. Once I got one phase done, I could start the next, which also had to be done in a timely fashion. Some of these processes could not be done until the one before it had been completed due to

43   HAR!

limited server capacity available for the work. So there was a lot of hurry up and wait involved. While it was churning along, I sometimes had one of my computer monitors displaying a web browser with the MSN homepage up just to follow any interesting developments in the world. One day, Colt stopped by my desk and suggested that I not do that, kind of like the way General Patton suggested that his troops not exhibit symptoms of shell-shock in the recovery ward (see the movie). Over time, I came to realize that Colt was the type of person who could go, seemingly at the flip of a switch, from being a jovial, personable guy to sending a contractor or vendor with whom he has an issue sailing out the front door with bite marks where their ass used to be, and then back to being his jolly, happy self again.

As it turned out, the inability to check the web wasn't a big problem for me, since I found that if I needed to see what was going on, I could just look across the row of cubicles from me. There were several individuals who were constantly online there, among them, another contractor who liked to shop for watches on Amazon, an employee from India who was a big fan of Cricket matches, and a guy whose ideological leanings were not dissimilar to my own who subscribed to the Drudge Report. The difference seemed to stem from the fact that this row of cubicles was along the route that Colt walked to get from his desk to the coffee machine, and so those screens were shielded from his line of sight. So, I was able to recognize that me being singled out for his wrath was a result of happenstance and not a question of discrimination in any way. Still, it bugged me a little, but I never said anything about it. Till now.

I have never had a problem with having a female boss, nor do I think that the possession of male genitalia automatically qualifies someone to be in charge. My friend Heywood Jablomie once said something that blew me away. (By the way, he pronounces his last name Ja-BLAH-mee. He says it rhymes with salami, which I think is like baloney.) Anyway, he said that even though it has been said that it is a man's world, the ugly truth is that women have always controlled it because they control the men. He maintains that it is hardly a stretch to say that there is practically nothing that a woman could want that she can't get a man to do for her if she gives him an inkling that she might make it worth his while. It makes you wonder who is really being exploited. That may sound sexist and cynical, but he insists it is an undeniable fact.

Many years ago, a book was written titled "Everything I Really Need to Know, I Learned in Kindergarten," by Robert Fulghum. There is a corollary to this thesis that goes "Everything I Really Need to Know, I Learned from Watching Star Trek." This show gave us many memorable observations, usually provided from the perspective of the extra-terrestrial member of the crew, Mr. Spock, such as, "you may find that having is not so satisfying a thing as wanting," or "curious how humans always manage to get that which they do not want," or "the needs of the many outweigh the needs of the few." There was a great episode of this show's original series in which Captain Kirk was involved in a freak mishap with the transporter beam and was split into two different versions of himself. One was based on his benevolent, good-hearted personality, and the other based on his darker side, characterized by greed, thirst for power, and lust for anything in a skirt. Once again, Spock, in his great wisdom, figured out that the wishy-washy Kirk was totally ineffectual without this baser nature driving him to accomplish what he wanted. It was only with the control and discipline of the good nature that he was a palatable human being. Perhaps that is a lesson in how to deal with managers.

One other intriguing Star Trek phenomenon was the legendary Orion slave girls, the green women who danced lasciviously for the appreciative eyes of captains and kings. They were introduced in the very first pilot episode of the franchise to point out that a respectable man, while inwardly wanting to get next to one, had to keep up appearances by resisting the urge to merge, if you will (damn, now I'm saying it). Near the finale of the franchise run that ended with the series "Enterprise," we are treated to another encounter with these women. This time, three of them are presented as a 'gift' to Captain Archer, and they begin to have their usual impact on the male members of the crew. It turned out that these women had themselves planted in that situation so that they could manipulate the crew in order to gain the upper hand in a trade negotiation or ruling the galaxy or some damn thing like that. Anyway, it was revealed to the good captain by the Orion trader that, indeed, it is the men who are the slaves in this system. A commentator on the show I read sometime after it aired was quite upset by the notion and blasted it as nothing more or less than victim blaming, but looking at it another way, you might conclude that Heywood has a point.

One of my all-time favorite Star Trek episodes was from the sixth season of the Next Generation series. The thing I admire most about the captain in this series, Jean-Luc Picard, is that he comes across as very cerebral. I'm sure it is no accident that Gene Roddenberry chose a contemplative, bald man for his captain when he rebooted the franchise, as the first criticism of the pilot episode of the original series is that it was too cerebral for the audience to understand. So, he reworked the concept, and the result was Captain James T. Kirk, who made it his mission to boldly kick ass where no ass has been kicked before.

In this episode, titled "Tapestry," Captain Picard suffers a near-death experience and finds himself in the presence of Q, the enigmatic, omnipresent, and quasi-superior being who takes perverse delight in pointing out to Picard the frailties of the human condition. In a retrospective on his life, the captain recalls an incident from his younger days where a brash decision resulted in a mishap which necessitated him receiving an artificial heart, which ultimately led to his 'death' in this story. Q offers him the opportunity to relive those days, and if he can avoid the situation that led to losing his heart, then he could live out the remainder of his natural life. Long story short, he succeeds in avoiding the injury, and Q happily returns him to his ship. Once there, however, Picard discovers that in this new reality he has never been and will never be the captain. Rather, he is a lieutenant for life, carrying reports to his superior officers and performing any other menial tasks they see fit. He questions the situation, and Q again appears to him and points out that this is the way his life would have turned out if he had not possessed the quality of impulsiveness that led to his injury. By playing it safe, he avoided situations where he would be thrust into taking bold steps and getting noticed. In this alternate reality, he never did get noticed and ended up everyone's doormat. Picard realizes his error and says he will take his chances on things turning out better from the situation as he recalls living it. He'd rather that than live the existence of a dreary man in a tedious job, having neither passion nor imagination as part of his life, and Q happily obliges him, letting him have his impulsive run-in with a surly alien, and suffering the consequences. As painful as the realization was for me, I had to admit that could be my story if you take away warp speed and energy-based weapons.

Part of the reason I ended up that way, it seems to me, is the fact of growing up in a family where I came along so late that my brothers were mostly grown up and on their own, starting families and building their lives. One of them had three sons who were just slightly younger than I am, so in a way, it felt like my nephews were more like my brothers than my actual brothers were. In addition, there were those who were openly hostile toward me as a kid, either because they perceived me as having advantages that they didn't, or just felt threatened by the possibility that I might not screw up my life like they did. There were just a lot of people who saw to it that I grew up in an environment where often was heard a discouraging word. If I would ever have the temerity to express any ambition, it would promptly be shot down. The experience was not unlike the kid in that Christmas movie who is constantly being told that he will shoot his eye out. So, I learned to keep my ambitions to myself and never really got good at standing my ground and fighting battles. It just seemed to make more sense to avoid conflict.

One aspect of my personality that I have come to realize is that I attempt to be a people pleaser. That is the main reason I started college in the first place. I knew my family would be happy to know I was making the effort, even if I didn't have a clear goal in mind. I have usually stayed with jobs longer than any self-respecting person would for the same reason. It was just easier if I felt I was making others happy.

You do need to exercise care in choosing a path to follow. In any field of endeavor, there are unscrupulous people who will try to take advantage of your desire to change your life. There isn't anyone who has a job that hasn't felt that they would like to leave and do something else at some time or another, and there are smooth operators out there who actively seek out people like this to make their livelihood. I am old enough to remember the old hustle of "make money from home by stuffing envelopes." This was promoted through classified ads in newspapers and magazines where you were told to send $1 to a PO box somewhere and learn about this great business opportunity. Although I never tried it myself, I heard that the way it worked was that you stuff $1 into an envelope and sent it off to this PO box. In a few days, you got back a letter containing instructions to get a PO box and take out a classified ad telling people to send $1 to your PO box and get instructions on how to make money from home stuffing envelopes. Nowadays, online entrepreneurs are plying a similar trade, but using more polish and sophistication, and it takes more than $1 to get the information on how to make money stuffing envelopes at home. Some of them have the germ of a good idea, but when it is all said and done, unless you come up with something that has real value to real people, you are never going to succeed in a business venture.

The biggest caution you must exercise in dealing with those who purport to help you achieve your goal of leaving the daily grind behind you is not to be pulled in by the scams that can be perpetrated. One of the primary ways they do this is to attempt to appeal to your feelings of greed and curiosity. These can be powerful agents in getting your attention, and you need to keep your guard up about things that sound too good to be true. After all, if these people were making a bundle doing what they were offering to teach you to do, wouldn't they be better off doing that rather than training their competition? In the 80s, the real estate gurus would ply people with the thought of being able to go to their bosses and telling them that either they could sell them the company or they would quit. Who wouldn't love to be able to say that?

Where Are They Now?

I thought it might be good to include a run-down of how some of the people with whom I have worked made out in subsequent years. The fact of the matter is that I am so far from giving a rat's ass about most of them that light reflecting off the rat's ass would take years to reach me. I could say that I take some comfort in knowing that time wounds all heels, but there are some that have gone through situations that I wouldn't wish on my worst enemy.

I caught up with Chris Chan a few years ago, and he told me that he had to transfer all of his operations to his home in order to keep going and had only a skeleton crew working for him. Shortly after I left, he and Marion had a baby boy, and it turned out that he had some health issues that nearly bankrupted them. I have to say, I really felt for them.

There was a time when I considered Austin Tayshus a good friend, but it seems that the feeling was not mutual. There were times when I would catch a glimpse of him at local sporting events, and he would not acknowledge my presence. I can only assume that he resented my relationship with Chris and the favor that he appeared to show me. As for Jacquelyn Hyde, she left the company to go to work, she said, as a cocktail server at a 'gentlemen's club' on the outskirts of town. To hear her tell it, she was only serving cocktails, but rumor has it that she fully embraced the gentlemen's club atmosphere. I have to admit, I never had any wish to see if that was the case.

Then there was the disturbing situation involving Ross Ewage from the TV station. One of the people I worked alongside became part owner of a movie theater, and once when Maxine and I went out to a movie, I struck up a conversation with him. He said that everyone was a little concerned about Ross because, one day, he just didn't show up for work. It was like he vanished without a trace. He had been missing for several days, so the station had no choice but to replace him. A week or two later, I picked up the newspaper and saw his picture, the article stated that he had been arrested by federal authorities and charged with running a child pornography server farm for an Internet group. Not long after that, I read that this 64-year-old man had been sentenced to 25 years in federal prison upon his conviction. That will teach him a lesson.

Several people I knew from the local office of LOT have moved on to bigger and better things. Some moved to other offices in the company and have kept in touch. Ida Wanda Godare still goes most anywhere they send her for software installations, and once she posted on social media that she was making a trip to the office I had been attached to at the end. I asked her to say hi to my friends there and also to Miss Management.

My mom was a survivor of bladder cancer for just over 22 years. I never regretted the time during those years that I put things on hold to be there for her and give whatever support I could. During the Fall Semester of my Junior year in college, she suddenly came down with cancer of the liver. We found out about it on November 1st and had her funeral on the 30th. Did I mention that November is not my favorite month?

My dad passed away about a year earlier, alone in his apartment. We had never had a warm relationship, but in recent years, I have moderated my feelings about why he was the way he was. We may never know the things that cause people to do the things they do or how it affects those closest to them. Still,

I was deeply saddened to hear of his passing. For about five minutes.

The Beginning of the End

The simple truth is that contractors are the rented mules of the workforce. Still, I have often had the feeling that a bad day in this job was better than a good day at LOT. As I mentioned earlier, the business is a Third-Party Administrator for businesses that operate self-funded benefit plans. When I started, my job involved arriving early in the morning to process the inbound health claims and loading them into the database, then maintaining the eligibility rolls and handling other various and sundry processing as needed. When the new CIO came on (and within two years had become CEO of the company), he wanted to change the perception of who we are as being an Integrated Health Management Company, and my job involved arriving early in the morning to process the inbound health claims and loading them into the database, then maintaining the eligibility rolls and handling other various and sundry processing as needed. Kind of like the movie "Groundhog Day" but with fewer festivities.

Near the end of my second year as a contractor here, I was told by my supervisor that they were ready to bring me on as a direct hire. They announced the fact at a department meeting to the crew that I, along with another individual who had been contracting for about six months, would be joining the company. That was going on a year ago, and the only change has been a lack of department status meetings. The fact is, they told a lot of people there about a lot of things that didn't happen. Not only that, but I overheard one of the administrative people while giving a client the grand tour of the office say that most of the tech people here are on contract because, that way, they don't have to do lay-offs if things slow down. Sadly, this is becoming the norm in the IT industry. In any case, I arrived at a very important conclusion about my willingness to continue working there as a contractor, as well as what I would advise anyone who wasn't my worst enemy about whether it is a great place to work, and that conclusion is how I arrived at the title of this chapter.

CONCLUSION

A great American once said, "the people who hate you don't win unless you hate them back."[44] I can honestly say that I don't hate anyone, it's against my religion (unfortunately, I sometimes have to remind people at church of that fact). That, however, is not a prohibition against strongly disliking certain individuals. I have known my share of difficult people over the years, and I have come to one inescapable conclusion; life will crush your spirit if you let it. I have chosen not to let it. If we give in to the ill will of those who seek to hold us down, then the terrorists will have won. I use the example of terrorists in the sense that terrorists are outlaws, and outlaws are synonymous with in-laws. Most of the in-laws I have struggled with are of the type who have been or are married to my brothers. One such individual, I have known since I was nine years old, and I have never been able to live up to her high standards. I used to shoulder the blame for this, but over the years, I have come to realize that she is just the type of person who wouldn't be happy if she didn't have something to be unhappy about (she probably wouldn't be happy with that sentence structure). She, and cohorts of her ilk, see only two kinds of people in the world, those who see things her way and those who need to be corrected. Curiously, the fact

44   Okay, it was Richard Nixon, but hang with me here.

that seemingly 99% of the population falls into the latter category doesn't seem to provide her with information about who could stand some correction.

What, then, is the answer for someone who has had it with struggling in a job and needs to find a new way to support themselves? There are those who will tell you to find something you enjoy and figure out how to monetize it. That can be easier said than done. What is a hobby you enjoy that could become a source of income? Perhaps you could teach others about it and make a side hustle out of that. One thing is certain; spending your productive life selling your time to an employer who doesn't share your values is the absolute worst way to eke out an existence. It results in long hours of looking forward to evenings and weekends, so wrapped up in making a living that you never have a life.

As I write this, it has been 20 years since I went back to school to finish the education that I started all those years ago, and I haven't regretted a day of it. The day I haven't regretted was yesterday, which I spent in a drunken stupor after signing off on the final edits to the manuscript of this book. Just kidding, I'm happy to report that I don't drink anymore. The obligatory joke there is I don't drink any less, but the fact is I can't drink like I used to, undoubtedly, because I drank like I used to. At the time, I would rationalize it by saying that after a week of dealing with the Ana/Talia tandem, by the time Friday rolled around, I needed something, but all I really needed was to remember the lessons taught by the good examples of bad examples around whom I grew up and determine not to go down that road.

Considering that I have earned (or at least been paid) well over half a million dollars more in the intervening years than I would have without a college degree, I have to say it was worth the few thousand dollars I had to borrow to obtain it. At least in a financial sense. Still, the longest employment stint that I maintained lasted 10 years, 8 months, and 23 days. That beat, by about three years, my run at the blue-collar factory job I did before I went back and finished my degree.

If I could have any do-overs, it would be to develop the knack of looking behind the scenes of what I was interested in to find things I could have pursued. The obvious battle is not always the real battle, just as the obvious opportunity is not always the real one. Like a lot of kids, I once fancied the notion of being a baseball player. Aside from the fact that I couldn't hit, or run, or throw, or catch the ball, I was a pretty good player, but I ultimately gave it up. It never occurred to me that there is more to baseball than being a player. What about scouting or sports writing, or working for a team doing statistics or marketing, or some other interesting aspect of the profession. Or software development. There are freelance programmers that do programs for businesses that have all kinds of worthy goals. There is also tutoring students to learn to write code or manage databases. There is a saying, he who can does, he who cannot teaches. That is a way of saying, you need to look for the thing within the thing that piques your interest and find a way to make it a livelihood.

A few years ago, I had the opportunity to attend a presentation by one of my childhood heroes. No, it wasn't Popeye the Sailor, but Frank the Astronaut. Frank Borman, the commander the first Apollo mission to fly to the moon happens to have a home not too far from where I live, and he was giving a talk at a banquet in my city. On his flight to the moon, he inspired millions with the memorable reading from the book of Genesis on Christmas Eve in 1968. In his talk at the event I attended, he stressed five main points that resulted in the success of the early space program and which could be adapted to other endeavors as well. These are:

1. Knowledge

   Many of the materials and techniques needed to reach outer space and the moon had not been developed at the time the decision was made to go there. There was a need to create these things on the fly. It has been observed that not many of the engineers in mission control had advanced degrees, they had B.S. degrees and a lot of common sense and the ability and willingness to roll up their sleeves and do what it took to get the job done.

2. Integrity

   Owning up to deficiencies and failure and not let them stand in the way. After the disastrous fire that took the lives of the Apollo 1 crew, everyone took an honest look at where they were and what needed to be corrected and got it working.

3. Mission

Knowing what you are trying to accomplish and figuring out what it will take to get there. This is what Napoleon Hill would call "definiteness of purpose" and is necessary in any attempt to accomplish great things.

4. Sacrifice

Investment in the future. All great achievements come at a cost. Determine what you are willing to give and the rewards you expect.

5. Risk

Nothing great can be accomplished without the possibility of failure. Don't be afraid to fail.

Mike Rowe, the host of the show "Dirty Jobs," gave a talk where he advises that rather than seek to make a living pursuing their passion that graduates should learn to become passionate about what they are doing. Yeah. Okay. Let me know how that works out for you.

There comes a point where you become less concerned about the career choices you make impacting your future. As your career path winds down to the point that you don't need to save as much for the future, you have more options to pursue jobs or activities that interest you rather than those that pay well. It can be nice to have both, but I would have gladly taken half what I was earning at LOT to have a sense of purpose and fulfillment, not to mention the ability to sleep at night.

The truth is that I have had the greatest sense of fulfillment from the tasks that I have performed for the network of support for families and helping Helen Highwater with the issues that confront her than I have from many of the assignments I have had at my real jobs over the years. Unfortunately, there hasn't been much in the way of remuneration from doing work for non-profit organizations. Helen did ask me once when I planned to go full-time with freelance programming work, and I told her that I would definitely need to pull down six figures to replace my current income given the fact I would have to pay my own health care and retirement program, plus both halves of Social Security. I asked how much of that could I put her down for? It never came up again. I guess that is the difference in thought processes between someone with a sociology degree and one with a business administration degree. One looks at the impact on people's lives, the other is concerned with the bottom line. They don't have a lot of money to invest in tech help, so I do what I can. I have had some second thoughts about my continued involvement with the program, but, as the saying goes, in the land of the blind, the one-eyed man is king.

Random Observations

The meek shall inherit the shit.

No one with whom I have ever worked has lost a minute of sleep over what kind of a mood I was going to be in when I got to the office the next day.

You may have noticed that I have included many anecdotes relating to our cats but none at all about my step-kids. Well, I have become convinced that there must be a special section of Heaven reserved for step-parents because they have already been through Hell. Another story for another day.

I have heard it said, and have come to believe, that when you wake up in the middle of the night and can't get back to sleep, it is God's way of saying to you, we need to talk, and you have time now.

It has occurred to me that my analogy of Captain Kirk may have been accurate in the sense that when a person can use their less attractive qualities to get results, it is an effective way to use directness as a motivator. It isn't always pleasant for the person on the receiving end, but it gets the job done.

People who have this type of directness and type-A mentality are almost never people who like cats. Some of history's most notable cat haters include Atilla the Hun, Napoleon, and Adolph Hitler among others. Those who are known to love cats are the likes of Mark Twain, Ernest Hemingway, and Albert Einstein. Just saying. Many of the people I have worked for who exhibit the typical boss mentality are not comfortable around cats and like to play up the tendencies of their dogs to eat cats. I agree with Mark Twain when he said that if you could cross-breed a human with a cat, it would improve the human but diminish the cat.

Some of the most effective bosses are people who would rather be feared than liked. They were critical of assistant managers who they saw as wanting to be buddies with the staff, as they felt it was not productive. They may have been right.

Final Thoughts

It is unfortunate that I wasn't able to hang in there in the situation I ended up in at LOT. When I was working directly for Ana and Darrell, my guiding principle was to be part of the solution rather than part of the problem. A big part of my resistance to the formality of filling out time tickets had to do with the fact that I often followed one of two approaches to completing a task. Either the Michelangelo approach, that is, it will be finished when I'm finished, or the Thomas Edison way, which is I'll have it solved when I run out of ideas that don't work. Either way, a lot of time can pass before I could deliver a satisfactory result. Maybe that is why Ana once said that managing programmers is like herding cats. As both a cat person and a programmer, I can agree with that assessment.

Captain Ahab was obsessed with bringing about the destruction of the white whale[45] that left him with a grievous injury that forever haunted him, but he didn't realize that this creature bore

45   AKA Moby Dick

him no malice or evil intent, it was simply living out its essential nature. Perhaps I am making the same mistake in my beliefs about Talia's intent[46]. It really is too bad that she took that approach because she lacked neither the intellect nor the personal magnetism needed to inspire people to put forth their best efforts for her. Unfortunately, she had a tremendous capacity for making the job feel like being in prison, only with less autonomy and empowerment.

If you believe you are the target of age discrimination, your best option is to point out to your supervisor the error of his or her ways and insist that they change. If, for some reason, that doesn't work out, you have several options available. You can

a) make like a tree and leave

b) make like a sheep herder and get the flock out

c) make like a bakery truck and haul buns out of there

Are you starting to see a theme develop here? Some would say good luck with that situation. I say, if you have taken stock of your abilities, talents, and aspirations, you can leverage them into a chance to realize your true purpose and calling, and in the process, make your own luck.

Recently, I have become acquainted with a writer named David Cook, a Sports Psychologist and author of the book "Golf's Sacred Journey," which he made into the movie "Seven Days

46   *Nah*

in Utopia." It is the story of a golfer who faced a crisis of identity and learned to use his career not as a vocation, but as a platform. I have spent some time with him in this small town in Texas called Utopia, a place not unlike Squaw Gap, North Dakota, except that it has paved roads, a golf course, and is an actual town. I have played golf with David on the course that was depicted in the movie, and I have left my buried lies in the cemetery there, not the least of which is the lie that I have to take what they're giving 'cuz I'm working for a living. David is a great believer in moving people from success to significance, and that there are few things more significant than helping people to find their way. I have learned that my identity issue is not so much a crisis but a chronic malaise, and that my recent career change was just one more instance of trading one bad situation for another, with very little chance of finding meaning, purpose, or significance from any of it.

I am convinced that God isn't done working on me. Those who have read to this point may not envy Him the task ahead, but I believe He can do it. There must be a reason for all the twists and turns life has taken over the years on that winding road. It is like looking at the meandering threads on the back side of a tapestry. You don't understand what you are supposed to be seeing, then you step out from behind it and see it in all its vibrancy. You are amazed at the intricacy of all those threads that formed it over the years, and you understand that everything is there for a reason, even (and perhaps, especially) the parts that made you turn and follow a different road. I realize now that every time I have done so, it has led to something of greater significance in my life. Ultimately, it resulted in the book you are now reading. So, I will continue along that road, confident that I will identify my true purpose and calling, and that the experiences I have had up till now will come to make sense in the tapestry of this life.

But for now, I have a tee time coming up.

Thanks for Reading

If you enjoyed this book, I would appreciate if you would leave a review here[47]

---

47 https://www.amazon.com/review/create-review/ref=cm_cr_othr_d_wr_but_ top?ie=UTF8&channel=glance-detail&asin=B07SDB6KYN

ACKNOWLEDGMENTS

I want to express my gratitude to my wife, Maxine (not her real name, but the letters in her real name could be rearranged to spell "tad un-leisurely"). She put up with my goofy schedules for years as well as the time I would lock myself away to work on this project.

My editor for this project inquired about the alternative names I gave the players in this story, and I had to say that it came from years of working with programmers who would set up databases for testing code and try to come up with the most outlandish names they could imagine. So, I can't say I came up with all of them on my own, but I contributed my share. Admittedly, there were some adult beverages involved, and many of the names were definitely not safe for work.

To David Cook, who has been the greatest inspiration to find my game and follow my true purpose and calling in life. Every time I return to the truths he teaches at www.linksofutopia. com, it makes me recommit to finding the thing that makes life worthwhile.

Finally, a big shout-out to Matt Stone, aka Buck Flogging, who took time out from his busy schedule as an Internet billionaire to notice my writing and offer encouragement, and, with the help of his company 100 Covers, designed the cover of this book. One down, 99 to go.

ABOUT THE AUTHOR

His biggest mistake was when he thought he was mistaken about something.

Double bogey is par for the course.

On a trip to San Antonio, he meant to visit the Alamo, but he forgot.

He is... one of the more intriguing guys around.

Mack Stout isn't always seething over the slings and arrows of outrageous BS, but when he is, he's maxed out. He prefers to leverage his edgy sense of humor to poke fun at situations that would make most people crazy (as if he's not). He takes his inspiration from the likes of Dave Barry, Patrick F. McManus, and Weird Al Yankovic, because these are people who seemingly have figured out how to not take themselves or much of anything else too seriously. He says that if he had figured out how to do that earlier in life, he would be far less neurotic than he is.

Mack spent close to 20 years in the software industry after graduating with a degree in Management Information Systems. After realizing that he was being called to a higher purpose than grinding out program code and toiling for those who can only see what they can take, he currently seeks to help those who find themselves dealing with unfulfilled potential in their lives.

Check out his blog at www.mackstout.com

Made in United States
North Haven, CT
26 May 2023

37015534R00115